LAND O LAKES®
COLLECTOR™ SERIES

Cookies

Versatile Butter Cookies, see page 52

Acknowledgments

LAND O LAKES® COLLECTOR™ SERIES

Land O'Lakes, Inc.
Lydia Botham, *Test Kitchens/Consumer Affairs Director*
Becky Wahlund, *Managing Food Editor*
Mary Sue Peterson, *Coordinating Food Editor*

Cy DeCosse Incorporated

Barry Benecke, *Creative Director*
Will Lotzow, *Senior Art Director*
Sandy Graff, *Senior Project Manager*
Maren Frevert, *Electronic Production*
Gretchen Gundersen, *Print Production Manager*

Tony Kubat Photography

Pictured on front cover: Jumbo Candy & Nut Cookies (page 44)

Recipes developed and tested by the Land O'Lakes Test Kitchens.

Reproduction in whole or part without written permission is prohibited.
All rights reserved. ©1994 Land O'Lakes, Inc.

Cookies.
p. cm. (Land O Lakes collector series)
Includes index.
ISBN 0-86573-954-4 (hardcover)   ISBN 0-86573-955-2 (softcover)
1. Cookies   I. Series.
TX772.C396 1994
641.8'654--dc20

PRINTED IN USA

Introduction

Cookies

There is nothing quite like a cookie to put a smile on your face and satisfy a sweet tooth. If Grandma's cookie jar was one of your favorite memories of growing up, then start reminiscing with the recipes in this volume of the LAND O LAKES® Collector™ Series.

We've even improved on the ideas from Grandma's day. Many are super-quick and easy to get you out of the kitchen sooner than Grandma ever did! Every recipe has been tested and retested by the professional home economists in our Land O'Lakes Test Kitchens. The easy-to-read, easy-to-follow format gives you a shortcut to success, one batch after another.

Try a new recipe every week— with the tempting ideas here, you'll have plenty of fun choosing. Start with "No-Bake Cookies & Bars" for a little something delicious and different. Don't miss the Chewy Candy Crunch Bars and Cherry Date Skillet Cookies. Move on to the second chapter, "Cookies," and you'll find everything from Grandma's Cookie Jar Oatmeal Cookies to Piña Colada Cookies. You'll also find wonderful chapters on "Bars," "Brownies" and "Holiday & Specialty Cookies & Bars."

With today's busy schedules, it's more important than ever to take time out to really enjoy life more. And why not consider a cookie as a necessary splurge, whether it's making cookies for a middle-of-the-day "pick-me-up" or an end-of-the-day reward? Leave it to Land O'Lakes to come up with the ideas for those melt-in-your-mouth moments you'll remember with a smile.

Table of Contents

Cookie-Making Questions & Answers 5

No-Bake Cookies & Bars 6

Cookies 24

Bars 54

Brownies 82

Holiday & Specialty Cookies & Bars 98

Index 126

Cookie-Making Questions & Answers

What kind of cookie sheet should I use for best results?

A shiny cookie sheet at least 2 inches narrower and shorter than the oven is best for evenly browned cookies. The sheet may be open on 1, 2 or 3 sides. Do not grease unless recipe states to do so. If a coated or dark cookie sheet is used, watch carefully for browning. Always place cookie dough on cool cookie sheets.

Where should I place cookie sheets in the oven during baking?

For evenly browned cookies, place 1 cookie sheet at a time on the center rack.

What can I do if my cookies stick to the cookie sheet?

Warm the cookies in the oven for 30 to 60 seconds; remove immediately. Use no stick cooking spray or shortening (not butter or margarine) to grease cookie sheets.

Why are my cookies spreading too much?

Cookies may be spreading too much for a variety of reasons. A test cookie will give a good indication of dough condition. Bake one cookie. If it spreads more than desired, the dough may be too soft. Try refrigerating dough until well chilled (1 to 2 hours). If the dough is still too soft, stir in 1 to 2 tablespoons flour. Do not oversoften the butter before making the dough. Also, do not use low-fat spreads (less than 70% fat) in place of butter. Low-fat spreads have a higher moisture content and cause cookie dough to be too soft. If you have used a low-fat spread, go ahead and bake the cookies rather than trying to "fix" the dough. Another way to prevent cookies from spreading too much is to be sure to cool cookie sheets completely before placing more cookie dough on them.

What is the best way to cool cookies if I do not have a wire cooling rack?

If you do not use a wire cooling rack to cool your cookies, they can become soft or soggy. To prevent this from happening, place a sheet of waxed paper on the counter and sprinkle it with granulated sugar. Place the cooling cookies on the sugared waxed paper.

How can I make soft cookies? Mine are always too crisp.

- ◆ Do not overbeat the dough once the dry ingredients have been mixed in. Overworking the dough will toughen the cookies.
- ◆ Do not overbake the cookies. They continue to set as they cool.
- ◆ Soft cookie doughs usually have more moisture than doughs for crisp cookies. If your dough looks dry, add 1 to 2 tablespoons of milk, cream, buttermilk or sour cream.
- ◆ Cake flour will give a more tender crumb to your baked cookies.
- ◆ Excess sugar often results in crisp, not soft, cookies.

No-Bake Cookies & Bars

Kids love to eat cookies and these no-bake treats make it extra easy—for mom too. Make quick-to-fix Chocolate Caramel & Nut Treats or Chewy Candy Crunch Bars for an easy snack or a special lunch box surprise.

Orange Butter Cream Squares, see page 8

Orange Butter Cream Squares

This creamy bar cookie combines two favorite flavors - orange and chocolate.

Preparation time: 30 minutes • Chilling time: 3 hours
(pictured on page 7)

Crust
- 1¼ cups (about 25) finely crushed chocolate wafer cookies
- ⅓ cup LAND O LAKES® Butter, softened

Filling
- 1½ cups powdered sugar
- ⅓ cup LAND O LAKES® Butter, softened
- 2 teaspoons grated orange peel
- 1 tablespoon milk
- ½ teaspoon vanilla

Glaze
- 1 tablespoon LAND O LAKES® Butter, melted
- 1 tablespoon unsweetened cocoa

In medium bowl stir together all crust ingredients. Press on bottom of 9-inch square pan. Cover; refrigerate until firm (1 hour).

In small mixer bowl combine all filling ingredients. Beat at medium speed, scraping bowl often, until creamy (3 to 4 minutes). Spread over crust.

In small bowl combine all glaze ingredients; drizzle over filling. Refrigerate until firm (1 to 2 hours). Cut into bars; store refrigerated. **YIELD:** 25 bars.

Nutrition Information (1 bar): Calories 90; Protein 1g; Carbohydrate 10g; Fat 6g; Cholesterol 15mg; Sodium 85mg

Butter Rum Almond Crunch

This quick and crunchy cookie has a delicious rum, caramel and marshmallow glaze for a sure-to-please family treat.

Preparation time: 15 minutes • Cooking time : 5 minutes

- ½ cup chopped maraschino cherries, well drained
- ¾ cup LAND O LAKES® Butter
- ½ cup firmly packed brown sugar
- 3 cups miniature marshmallows*
- 6 cups crisp rice cereal
- 1 (2½-ounce) package (⅔ cup) sliced almonds
- 1 teaspoon rum extract

Wrap drained cherries in paper towel to absorb any extra moisture. In 3-quart saucepan combine butter and brown sugar. Cook over medium heat, stirring constantly, until butter is melted and brown sugar is dissolved (4 to 5 minutes). Stir in marshmallows; continue cooking, stirring constantly, until marshmallows are melted (1 to 2 minutes). Remove from heat; stir in cherries and all remaining ingredients. Spread mixture into buttered 13x9-inch pan. Cool completely; cut into bars. **YIELD:** 36 bars.

* 30 large marshmallows can be substituted for 3 cups miniature marshmallows.

Nutrition Information (1 bar): Calories 90; Protein 1g; Carbohydrate 11g; Fat 5g; Cholesterol 10mg; Sodium 100mg

Cherry Date Skillet Cookies

Snowy coconut coats these made-in-the-skillet, buttery date cookies.

Preparation time: 40 minutes • Cooking time: 5 minutes

- 1 cup LAND O LAKES® Butter
- 1 cup firmly packed brown sugar
- 1 (8-ounce) package chopped dates
- 1 egg
- 3 cups crisp rice cereal
- 1 cup flaked coconut
- ½ cup chopped maraschino cherries, drained
- 1 tablespoon vanilla

- 2½ cups flaked coconut

In 10-inch skillet melt butter over medium heat. Stir in sugar and dates; remove from heat. Stir in egg; return to heat. Cook over medium heat, stirring constantly, until mixture comes to a full boil (4 to 6 minutes). Boil, stirring constantly, 1 minute. Remove from heat; stir in all remaining ingredients <u>except</u> 2½ cups coconut until moistened. Let stand 10 minutes. Shape rounded teaspoonfuls into 1-inch balls; roll in coconut. **YIELD:** 5 dozen cookies.

Nutrition Information (1 cookie): Calories 80; Protein 1g; Carbohydrate 10g; Fat 5g; Cholesterol 10mg; Sodium 50mg

Chocolate Caramel & Nut Treats

*Popular caramel, chocolate and peanuts combine to make
a treat kids of all ages will enjoy.*

Preparation time: 15 minutes • Cooking time: 8 minutes

- 12 double (5x2½-inch) graham crackers
- ¾ cup firmly packed brown sugar
- ¾ cup LAND O LAKES® Butter
- 1 (6-ounce) package (1 cup) semi-sweet real chocolate chips
- 1 cup salted peanuts

Line 15x10x1-inch jelly roll pan with graham crackers. In 2-quart saucepan combine sugar and butter. Cook over medium heat, stirring occasionally, until mixture comes to a full boil (3 to 5 minutes). Boil, stirring constantly, 5 minutes. Immediately pour over graham crackers; spread to coat. Sprinkle with chocolate chips. Let stand 1 minute; spread chocolate chips. Sprinkle with peanuts; lightly press peanuts into chocolate. Cool completely; break into pieces. **YIELD:** 48 bars.

*Nutrition Information (1 bar): Calories 100; Protein 1g; Carbohydrate 11g; Fat 6g;
Cholesterol 10mg; Sodium 110mg*

Chewy Candy Crunch Bars

A chewy caramel coats crisp cereal in this sure-to-please bar.

Preparation time: 20 minutes • Cooking time: 5 minutes

4	cups bite-size crispy corn cereal squares
1	cup salted peanuts
1	(8-ounce) package (1 cup) candy coated milk chocolate pieces
½	cup LAND O LAKES® Butter
1	cup firmly packed brown sugar
½	cup light corn syrup
2	tablespoons all-purpose flour

In large bowl combine cereal, peanuts and candies; set aside. In 2-quart saucepan melt butter (2 to 4 minutes). Stir in all remaining ingredients. Cook over medium heat, stirring occasionally, until mixture comes to a full boil (2 to 4 minutes). Boil 1 minute. Pour over cereal mixture; toss to coat well. Press on bottom of buttered 13x9-inch pan. Cool completely; cut into bars. **YIELD:** 36 bars.

Nutrition Information (1 bar): Calories 130; Protein 2g; Carbohydrate 18g; Fat 6g; Cholesterol 8mg; Sodium 100mg

Chewy Candy Crunch Bars; Chocolate-Topped Crunchy Cereal Bars, see page 16

Chocolate-Topped Crunchy Cereal Bars

Immediately sprinkle chocolate chips over the hot cereal mixture for an easy chocolate frosting.

Preparation time: 20 minutes • Cooking time: 10 minutes • Chilling time: 30 minutes
(pictured on page 15)

- 1 cup sugar
- ½ cup all-purpose flour
- ½ cup LAND O LAKES® Butter
- ⅔ cup light corn syrup
- ⅓ cup milk
- 4 cups toasted graham cereal squares
- 3 cups crisp rice cereal
- 1 cup salted peanuts
- 1½ cups semi-sweet real chocolate chips

In 6-quart Dutch oven combine sugar, flour, butter, corn syrup and milk. Cook over medium heat, stirring occasionally, until mixture comes to a full boil (5 to 8 minutes). Boil, stirring constantly, 5 minutes. Remove from heat; stir in cereals and peanuts until well coated. Spread into 13x9-inch pan. Immediately sprinkle with chocolate chips. Let stand 4 minutes; spread chocolate chips. Cover; refrigerate until firm (at least 30 minutes). Cut into bars.
YIELD: 36 bars.

Nutrition Information (1 bar): Calories 150; Protein 2g; Carbohydrate 21g; Fat 7g; Cholesterol 7mg; Sodium 130mg

No-Bake Chocolate Cookies

An easy ending to a quick meal.

Preparation time: 20 minutes • Cooking time: 3 minutes

1½ cups quick-cooking oats
½ cup flaked coconut
¼ cup chopped walnuts
¾ cup sugar
¼ cup milk
¼ cup LAND O LAKES® Butter
3 tablespoons unsweetened cocoa

In medium bowl combine oats, coconut and walnuts; set aside. In 2-quart saucepan combine sugar, milk, butter and cocoa. Cook over medium heat, stirring occasionally, until mixture comes to a full boil (3 to 4 minutes). Remove from heat; stir in oat mixture. Quickly drop by rounded teaspoonfuls onto waxed paper. Cool completely; store refrigerated. **YIELD:** 2 dozen cookies.

Nutrition Information (1 cookie): Calories 80; Protein 1g; Carbohydrate 11g; Fat 4g; Cholesterol 5mg; Sodium 26mg

No-Bake Rocky Road Chocolate Bars

Only six ingredients are in these no-bake bars.

Preparation time: 15 minutes • Cooking time: 4 minutes • Chilling time: 30 minutes

- ½ cup LAND O LAKES® Butter
- 1 (12-ounce) package (2 cups) semi-sweet real chocolate chips
- 1 cup butterscotch-flavored chips
- 1 cup peanut butter
- 4 cups crisp rice cereal
- 3 cups miniature marshmallows

In Dutch oven combine butter, chocolate chips and butterscotch chips. Cook over low heat, stirring constantly, until melted (4 to 6 minutes). Stir in peanut butter until well mixed. Remove from heat; stir in cereal and marshmallows until well coated. Press on bottom of buttered 13x9-inch pan. Refrigerate until firm (about 30 minutes). Cut into bars; store refrigerated. **YIELD:** 36 bars.

Nutrition Information (1 bar): Calories 160; Protein 3g; Carbohydrate 15g; Fat 11g; Cholesterol 5mg; Sodium 110mg

Peanut Butter Chocolate Granola Bars

Two favorite flavors, peanut butter and chocolate, combine with peanuts and raisins in this easy no-bake bar.

Preparation time: 15 minutes • Cooking time: 4 minutes • Chilling time: 1 hour

2½   cups granola cereal
½   cup coarsely chopped salted peanuts
½   cup raisins
1½   cups semi-sweet real chocolate chips
¼   cup peanut butter
¼   cup light corn syrup

In large bowl stir together cereal, peanuts and raisins. In 1-quart saucepan combine chocolate chips, peanut butter and corn syrup. Cook over low heat, stirring occasionally, until chocolate chips are melted and mixture is smooth (4 to 6 minutes). Pour over cereal mixture; toss to coat. Press on bottom of buttered 9-inch square pan. Cover; refrigerate until firm (about 1 hour). Cut into bars; store refrigerated. **YIELD:** 25 bars.

Nutrition Information (1 bar): Calories 170; Protein 3g; Carbohydrate 160g; Fat 10g; Cholesterol 0mg; Sodium 40mg

Microwave Toffee Bars

*Chocolate and peanut butter team up in this
easy microwave recipe.*

Preparation time: 20 minutes • Microwave time: 8 minutes • Chilling time: 1 hour 30 minutes

5½	double (5x2½-inch) graham crackers
1	cup (6 double 5x2½-inch) crushed graham crackers
¾	cup sugar
½	cup firmly packed brown sugar
½	cup LAND O LAKES® Butter
⅓	cup milk
½	cup semi-sweet real chocolate chips
¼	cup chunky-style peanut butter

Line bottom of buttered 12x8-inch baking dish with graham crackers; set aside. In 2-quart casserole combine all remaining ingredients except chocolate chips and peanut butter. Microwave on HIGH, stirring after half the time, until mixture comes to a full boil (2 to 2½ minutes). Microwave on HIGH 5 minutes (mixture will be very hot). Immediately pour mixture evenly over crackers. In 2-cup glass measure combine chocolate chips and peanut butter. Microwave on HIGH until chocolate is softened (45 to 60 seconds). Stir until smooth and melted. Spread evenly over toffee mixture; refrigerate until chocolate is set (at least 1½ hours). Cut into bars; store at room temperature. **YIELD:** 32 bars.

Nutrition Information (1 bar): Calories 100; Protein 1g; Carbohydrate 14g; Fat 5g; Cholesterol 10mg; Sodium 75mg

Peppermint N' Chocolate Bars

Refreshing peppermint complements chocolate in these easy-to-make bars.

Preparation time: 20 minutes • Cooking time: 3 minutes • Chilling time: 2 hours 30 minutes

Crust
- ½ cup LAND O LAKES® Butter
- ½ cup sugar
- ⅓ cup unsweetened cocoa
- 1 teaspoon vanilla
- 1½ cups graham cracker crumbs
- 1 cup flaked coconut
- ½ cup chopped nuts

Filling
- 2 cups powdered sugar
- ½ cup LAND O LAKES® Butter, softened
- 2 tablespoons milk
- 1 teaspoon peppermint extract
- 3 drops red <u>or</u> green food coloring, if desired

Frosting
- ⅓ cup semi-sweet real chocolate chips
- 1 teaspoon vegetable oil

In 2-quart saucepan combine butter, sugar, cocoa and vanilla. Cook over medium heat, stirring constantly, until butter is melted and mixture is smooth (1 to 2 minutes). Stir in all remaining crust ingredients. Press firmly on bottom of 13x9-inch pan. Refrigerate until firm (15 to 20 minutes).

In small mixer bowl combine all filling ingredients. Beat at medium speed, scraping bowl often, until smooth (2 to 3 minutes). Spread evenly over crust; refrigerate 15 minutes.

In 1-quart saucepan melt chocolate chips and oil over low heat, stirring constantly, until chocolate is smooth (2 to 4 minutes). Drizzle evenly over bars. Cover; refrigerate until firm (2 to 3 hours). Cut into bars; store refrigerated. **YIELD:** 48 bars.

Nutrition Information (1 bar): Calories 90; Protein 1g; Carbohydrate 10g; Fat 6g; Cholesterol 10mg; Sodium 60mg

Peanut Butter No-Bake Cookies

These quick & easy drop cookies have only five ingredients.

Preparation time: 20 minutes • Cooking time: 4 minutes

- ½ cup chunky-style peanut butter
- ¼ cup LAND O LAKES® Butter
- 15 large marshmallows*
- 1 cup quick-cooking oats
- ½ cup flaked coconut

    Flaked coconut, if desired

In 2-quart saucepan combine peanut butter, butter and marshmallows. Cook over medium heat, stirring constantly, until marshmallows are melted (4 to 7 minutes). Remove from heat; stir in oats and ½ cup coconut. Quickly drop by rounded teaspoonfuls onto waxed paper. Cool completely. Cover; store refrigerated. If desired, while cookies are warm roll in additional coconut. **YIELD:** 2 dozen cookies.

* 1½ cups miniature marshmallows can be substituted for 15 large marshmallows.

Nutrition Information (1 cookie): Calories 80; Protein 2g; Carbohydrate 8g; Fat 5g; Cholesterol 5mg; Sodium 50mg

Cookies

The bottom of the cookie jar will appear all too soon when you bake a batch of these favorites. Indulge in every sweet sensation imaginable— yummy Banana Cream Sandwich Cookies, Nutty Chocolate Chunk Cookies and Tart N' Tangy Lemonade Frosties. Everyone will be asking for your recipes.

Honey Gems, see page 26; Cheery Cherry Macaroons, see page 27

Honey Gems

These hearty cookies are flavored with a touch of orange.

Preparation time: 1 hour 15 minutes • Baking time: 8 minutes
(pictured on page 25)

Cookies

1½	cups all-purpose flour
½	cup quick-cooking oats
¼	cup sesame seed
¼	cup wheat germ
⅔	cup LAND O LAKES® Butter, softened
½	cup honey
¼	cup orange juice
1	egg
½	teaspoon salt
¼	teaspoon baking soda
1	tablespoon grated orange peel
1	teaspoon vanilla

Frosting

¾	cup powdered sugar
¼	cup LAND O LAKES® Butter, softened
1	teaspoon grated orange peel
2	teaspoons orange juice

Heat oven to 350°. In large mixer bowl combine all cookie ingredients. Beat at low speed, scraping bowl often, until well mixed (1 to 2 minutes). Drop by rounded teaspoonfuls 2 inches apart onto cookie sheets. Bake for 8 to 12 minutes or until edges are lightly browned.

Meanwhile, in small mixer bowl combine all frosting ingredients. Beat at medium speed, scraping bowl often, until creamy (1 to 2 minutes). Frost warm cookies. **YIELD:** 4 dozen cookies.

TIP: If desired, do not frost.

Nutrition Information (1 cookie): Calories 70; Protein 1g; Carbohydrate 9g; Fat 4g; Cholesterol 15mg; Sodium 65mg

Cheery Cherry Macaroons

This macaroon-type cookie is filled with cherries and nuts.

Preparation time: 1 hour • Baking time: 15 minutes
(pictured on page 25)

- 3 cups all-purpose flour
- 1 cup sugar
- 1 cup LAND O LAKES® Butter, softened
- ¼ cup milk
- 1 egg
- 1 teaspoon baking powder
- ¼ teaspoon salt
- 1 teaspoon almond extract
- ½ cup chopped pecans
- ½ cup maraschino cherries, chopped, well drained

- 2 cups flaked coconut

Heat oven to 350°. In large mixer bowl combine all ingredients <u>except</u> pecans, maraschino cherries and coconut. Beat at low speed, scraping bowl often, until well mixed (2 to 3 minutes). By hand, stir in pecans and maraschino cherries. Drop rounded teaspoonfuls of dough into coconut; roll into 1-inch balls. Place 1 inch apart on cookie sheets. Bake for 15 to 20 minutes or until lightly browned (coconut will be toasted). Let stand 1 minute; remove from cookie sheets. Store in tightly covered container. **YIELD:** 4 dozen cookies.

Nutrition Information (1 cookie): Calories 110; Protein 1g; Carbohydrate 12g; Fat 6g; Cholesterol 15mg; Sodium 60mg

Banana Cream Sandwich Cookies

These banana cookies are fun to make and are filled with a buttery frosting for a delicious sandwich cookie.

Preparation time: 1 hour 15 minutes • Baking time: 12 minutes • Cooling time: 15 minutes

Cookies
- 2 1/3 cups all-purpose flour
- 1 cup sugar
- 1 cup LAND O LAKES® Butter, softened
- 1 medium (1/2 cup) banana, sliced 1/4-inch
- 1/4 teaspoon salt
- 1 teaspoon vanilla
- 1/2 cup chopped pecans

Frosting
- 3 cups powdered sugar
- 1/3 cup LAND O LAKES® Butter, softened
- 1 teaspoon vanilla
- 3 to 4 tablespoons milk

  Food coloring

Heat oven to 350°. In large mixer bowl combine all cookie ingredients except pecans. Beat at low speed, scraping bowl often, until well mixed (2 to 3 minutes). By hand, stir in pecans. Shape rounded teaspoonfuls of dough into 1-inch balls. Place 2 inches apart on greased cookie sheets. Flatten balls to 1/4-inch thickness with bottom of buttered glass dipped in flour. Bake for 12 to 15 minutes or until edges are lightly browned. Remove from cookie sheets immediately; cool completely.

In small mixer bowl combine all frosting ingredients except milk and food coloring. Beat at medium speed, scraping bowl often and gradually adding enough milk for desired spreading consistency. If desired, color frosting with food coloring. Put cookies together in pairs with 1 tablespoonful filling for each sandwich.
YIELD: 2 dozen cookies.

Nutrition Information (1 cookie): Calories 240; Protein 2g; Carbohydrate 31g; Fat 12g; Cholesterol 30mg; Sodium 130mg

Buttery Toffee Cookies

Chocolate coated toffee makes these cookies extra good.

Preparation time: 1 hour • Baking time: 10 minutes

½ cup sugar
½ cup LAND O LAKES® Butter, softened
1 egg
½ teaspoon vanilla
1¼ cups all-purpose flour
½ teaspoon baking soda
½ teaspoon salt
4 (1.4-ounce) bars chocolate coated toffee, chopped*

Heat oven to 350°. In large mixer bowl combine sugar, butter, egg and vanilla. Beat at medium speed, scraping bowl often, until creamy (3 to 4 minutes). Reduce speed to low; add flour, baking soda and salt. Continue beating, scraping bowl often, until well mixed (1 to 2 minutes). By hand, stir in chopped toffee. Drop by rounded teaspoonfuls onto greased cookie sheets. Bake for 10 to 12 minutes or until lightly browned. Cool 1 minute; remove from cookie sheets. **YIELD:** 4 dozen cookies.

*1 (6-ounce) package (1 cup) toffee bits can be substituted for 4 (1.4-ounce) bars chocolate coated toffee, chopped.

Nutrition Information (1 cookie): Calories 60; Protein 1g; Carbohydrate 6g; Fat 3g; Cholesterol 10mg; Sodium 65mg

Chewy Jumbo Chocolate Chip Cookies

The addition of cake flour helps make these cookies soft and chewy.

Preparation time: 45 minutes • Baking time: 10 minutes

- 3¼ cups all-purpose flour
- 1 cup cake flour*
- 1 teaspoon baking powder
- 1 teaspoon baking soda
- 1¼ cups sugar
- 1¼ cups firmly packed brown sugar
- 1½ cups LAND O LAKES® Butter, softened
- 2 eggs
- 1 tablespoon vanilla
- 1 (12-ounce) package (2 cups) semi-sweet real chocolate chips <u>or</u> chunks

Heat oven to 375°. In medium bowl combine flour, cake flour, baking powder and baking soda; set aside. In large mixer bowl combine sugar, brown sugar and butter. Beat at medium speed, scraping bowl often, until creamy (2 to 3 minutes). Add eggs and vanilla. Continue beating, scraping bowl often, until well mixed (1 minute). Reduce speed to low. Continue beating, gradually adding flour mixture, until well mixed (2 to 3 minutes). By hand, stir in chocolate chips. Drop dough by ¼ cupfuls 2 inches apart onto cookie sheets. Bake for 10 to 14 minutes or until light golden brown. (DO NOT OVERBAKE.) Let stand 1 to 2 minutes; remove from cookie sheets. **YIELD:** 26 jumbo cookies.

* 1 cup minus 2 tablespoons all-purpose flour can be substituted for 1 cup cake flour. (Cookies will be flat and less chewy.)

TIP: For 2½-inch cookies, drop dough by rounded tablespoonfuls 2 inches apart onto cookie sheets. Bake for 10 to 12 minutes or until light golden brown. YIELD: 4 dozen cookies.

Nutrition Information (1 cookie): Calories 310; Protein 3g; Carbohydrate 42g; Fat 16g; Cholesterol 45mg; Sodium 170mg

Buttery Pistachio Cookies

A delicious butter cookie filled with chopped pistachios.

Preparation time: 1 hour • Chilling time: 1 hour • Baking time: 10 minutes

1 cup sugar
1 cup LAND O LAKES® Butter, softened
2 eggs
2 teaspoons vanilla
2 3/4 cups all-purpose flour
1 cup (5 ounces) finely chopped salted pistachios, toasted
1/4 teaspoon salt

1 egg white
1 tablespoon water
1/4 cup (1 1/2 ounces) finely chopped salted pistachios, toasted

In large mixer bowl combine sugar and butter. Beat at medium speed, scraping bowl often, until creamy (1 to 2 minutes). Add 2 eggs and vanilla. Continue beating, scraping bowl often, until well mixed (1 to 2 minutes). Reduce speed to low; add flour, 1 cup pistachios and salt. Continue beating, scraping bowl often, until well mixed (1 to 2 minutes). Divide dough in half; wrap in plastic food wrap. Refrigerate until firm (at least 1 hour).

Heat oven to 350°. On lightly floured surface roll out dough, half at a time (keeping remaining dough refrigerated), to 1/4-inch thickness. Cut with 2 1/2-inch round cookie cutter; cut each round in half. Place 1 inch apart on greased cookie sheets.

In small bowl beat together egg white and water. Brush tops of cookies lightly with egg mixture; sprinkle with 1/4 cup chopped pistachios. Bake for 10 to 12 minutes or until edges are lightly browned.
YIELD: 6 dozen cookies.

Nutrition Information (1 cookie): Calories 70; Protein 1g; Carbohydrate 7g; Fat 4g; Cholesterol 15mg; Sodium 35mg

Cashew Butter Cookies

Salted cashew halves are an attractive topping for these buttery cookies.

Preparation time: 1 hour • Baking time: 6 minutes

- ¾ cup LAND O LAKES® Butter, softened
- ½ cup firmly packed brown sugar
- ½ cup honey
- 1 egg
- 2 cups all-purpose flour
- ¾ teaspoon baking soda
- ½ teaspoon baking powder
- 1 cup chopped salted cashews

  Salted cashew halves

Heat oven to 375°. In large mixer bowl combine butter, sugar, honey and egg. Beat at medium speed, scraping bowl often, until well mixed (1 to 2 minutes). Reduce speed to low. Add all remaining ingredients <u>except</u> chopped cashews and cashew halves. Continue beating, scraping bowl often, until well mixed (1 to 2 minutes). By hand, stir in chopped cashews. Drop by rounded teaspoonfuls onto cookie sheets; top each cookie with cashew half. Bake for 6 to 9 minutes or until golden brown. **YIELD:** 4½ dozen cookies.

Nutrition Information (1 cookie): Calories 80; Protein 1g; Carbohydrate 9g; Fat 4g; Cholesterol 10mg; Sodium 70mg

Cashew Butter Cookies; Piña Colada Cookies, see page 36

Piña Colada Cookies

*Pineapple and coconut combine with a hint
of rum for a delicious cookie.*

Preparation time: 1 hour 30 minutes • Baking time: 8 minutes • Cooling time: 15 minutes
(pictured on page 35)

Cookies
- 1/2 cup sugar
- 1/3 cup LAND O LAKES® Butter, softened
- 1/3 cup pineapple preserves
- 2 eggs
- 1/2 teaspoon baking powder
- 1/2 teaspoon salt
- 1/2 teaspoon rum extract
- 1 3/4 cups all-purpose flour
- 1/4 cup flaked coconut

Frosting
- 3/4 cup powdered sugar
- 1/4 cup LAND O LAKES® Butter, softened
- 1 teaspoon water
- 1/4 teaspoon rum extract

Toasted coconut, if desired

Heat oven to 350°. In large mixer bowl combine all cookie ingredients except flour and coconut. Beat at low speed, scraping bowl often, until well mixed (1 to 2 minutes). By hand, stir in flour and coconut until well mixed. Drop dough by rounded teaspoonfuls 2 inches apart onto greased cookie sheets. Bake for 8 to 12 minutes or until edges are lightly browned. Cool completely.

In small mixer bowl combine all frosting ingredients except toasted coconut. Beat at medium speed, scraping bowl often, until creamy (1 to 2 minutes). Frost cooled cookies; sprinkle with toasted coconut. **YIELD:** 3 dozen cookies.

*Nutrition Information (1 cookie): Calories 90; Protein 1g; Carbohydrate 12g; Fat 4g;
Cholesterol 20mg; Sodium 70mg*

Hermits

An old-fashioned cookie made with molasses.

Preparation time: 1 hour • Baking time: 10 minutes

- 2 cups all-purpose flour
- 1 cup sugar
- ¾ cup LAND O LAKES® Butter, softened
- ¼ cup molasses
- 1 egg
- 1 teaspoon baking soda
- ½ teaspoon salt
- ½ teaspoon cloves
- ½ teaspoon ginger
- ½ cup raisins
- ½ cup chopped walnuts or pecans

Heat oven to 350°. In large mixer bowl combine all ingredients except raisins and walnuts. Beat at low speed, scraping bowl often, until well mixed (2 to 3 minutes). By hand, stir in raisins and walnuts. Drop dough by tablespoonfuls 2 inches apart onto cookie sheets. Bake for 10 to 12 minutes or until set. Let stand 1 minute; remove from cookie sheets. **YIELD:** 3½ dozen cookies.

Nutrition Information (1 cookie): Calories 90; Protein 1g; Carbohydrate 12g; Fat 4g; Cholesterol 15mg; Sodium 90mg

Citrus Slice N' Bake Cookies

The flavors of orange and lemon shine in these delicate butter cookies.

Preparation time: 1 hour 15 minutes • Chilling time: 2 hours • Baking time: 7 minutes

Cookies
- 2 cups all-purpose flour
- 1¼ cups powdered sugar
- ¾ cup LAND O LAKES® Butter, softened
- 1 egg
- 1 teaspoon baking powder
- ½ teaspoon salt
- ¼ teaspoon baking soda
- 1 teaspoon grated orange peel
- 2 teaspoons lemon extract

Sugar
- ¼ cup sugar
- 4 drops yellow food coloring
- 2 drops red food coloring

- 2 tablespoons LAND O LAKES® Butter, melted

In large mixer bowl combine all cookie ingredients. Beat at low speed, scraping bowl often, until well mixed (2 to 3 minutes). Divide dough in half; shape each half into 6-inch roll (about 1½-inch diameter). Wrap in plastic food wrap; refrigerate at least 2 hours.

Meanwhile, in medium jar with lid combine sugar and yellow food coloring; cover. Shake until well blended (1 to 2 minutes). Remove 2 tablespoons colored sugar; add red food coloring to remaining sugar. Cover; shake until well blended (1 to 2 minutes).

<u>Heat oven to 375°</u>. Cut rolls in half lengthwise; brush with melted butter. Roll 2 halves in yellow sugar and 2 halves in orange sugar. Cut rolls into ¼-inch slices. Place 1 inch apart on cookie sheets. Bake for 7 to 10 minutes or until edges are lightly browned.
YIELD: 4 dozen cookies.

Nutrition Information (1 cookie): Calories 60; Protein 1g; Carbohydrate 8g; Fat 4g; Cholesterol 15mg; Sodium 70mg

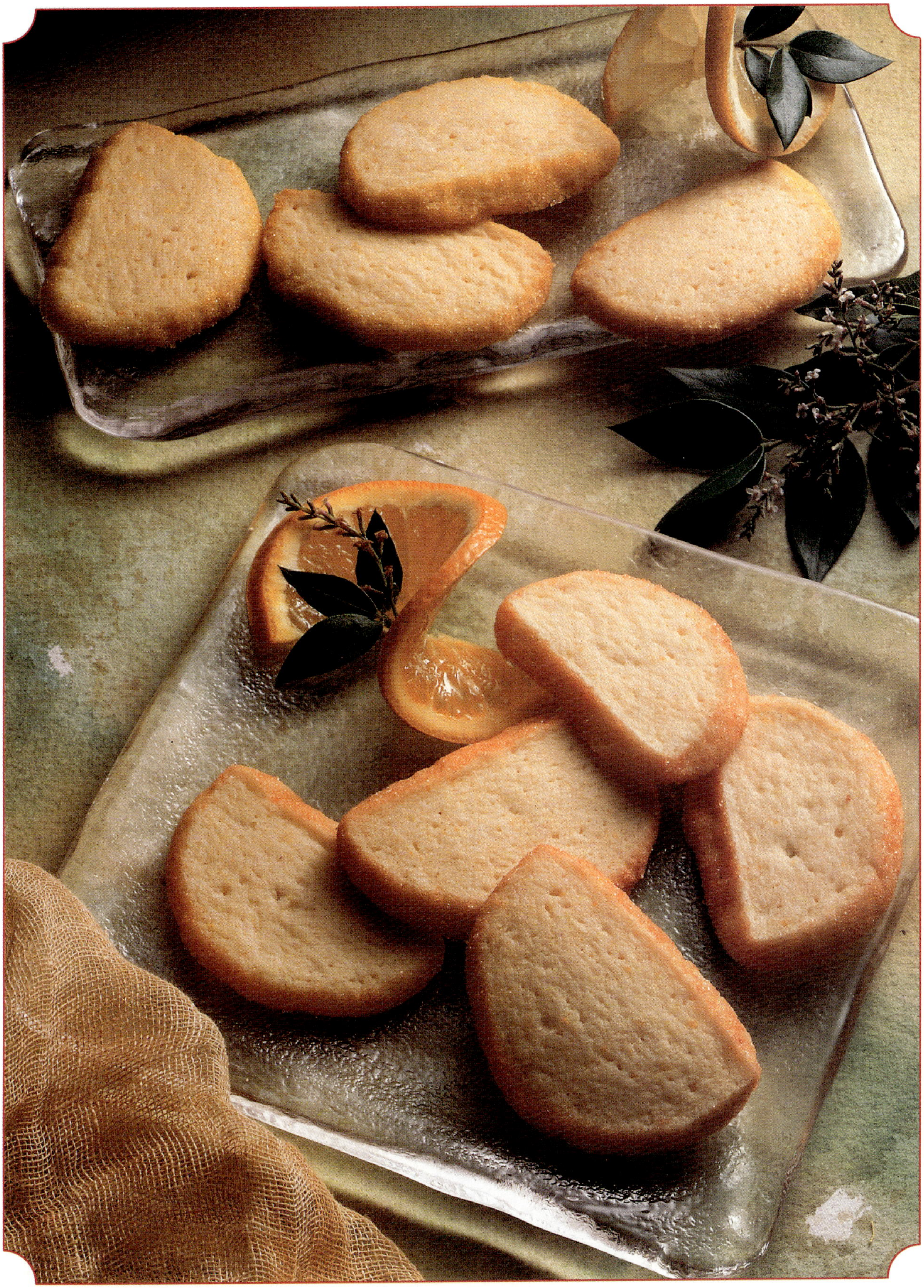

Grandma's Cookie Jar Oatmeal Cookies

These tasty, chewy cookies will remind you of Grandma's always-full cookie jar.

Preparation time: 50 minutes • Baking time: 8 minutes

- 3 cups quick-cooking oats
- 2 cups firmly packed brown sugar
- 1 cup LAND O LAKES® Butter, softened
- 2 eggs
- 1 teaspoon baking soda
- 1 teaspoon cinnamon
- ½ teaspoon salt
- 2 teaspoons vanilla
- 1¾ cups all-purpose flour
- 1½ cups raisins

Heat oven to 375°. In large mixer bowl combine all ingredients <u>except</u> flour and raisins. Beat at low speed, scraping bowl often, until well mixed (1 to 2 minutes). Add flour; continue beating until well mixed (1 to 2 minutes). By hand, stir in raisins. Drop by rounded teaspoonfuls 2 inches apart onto greased cookie sheets. Bake for 8 to 10 minutes or until edges are lightly browned. **YIELD:** 4 dozen cookies.

Nutrition Information (1 cookie): Calories 120; Protein 2g; Carbohydrate 19g; Fat 4g; Cholesterol 20mg; Sodium 90mg

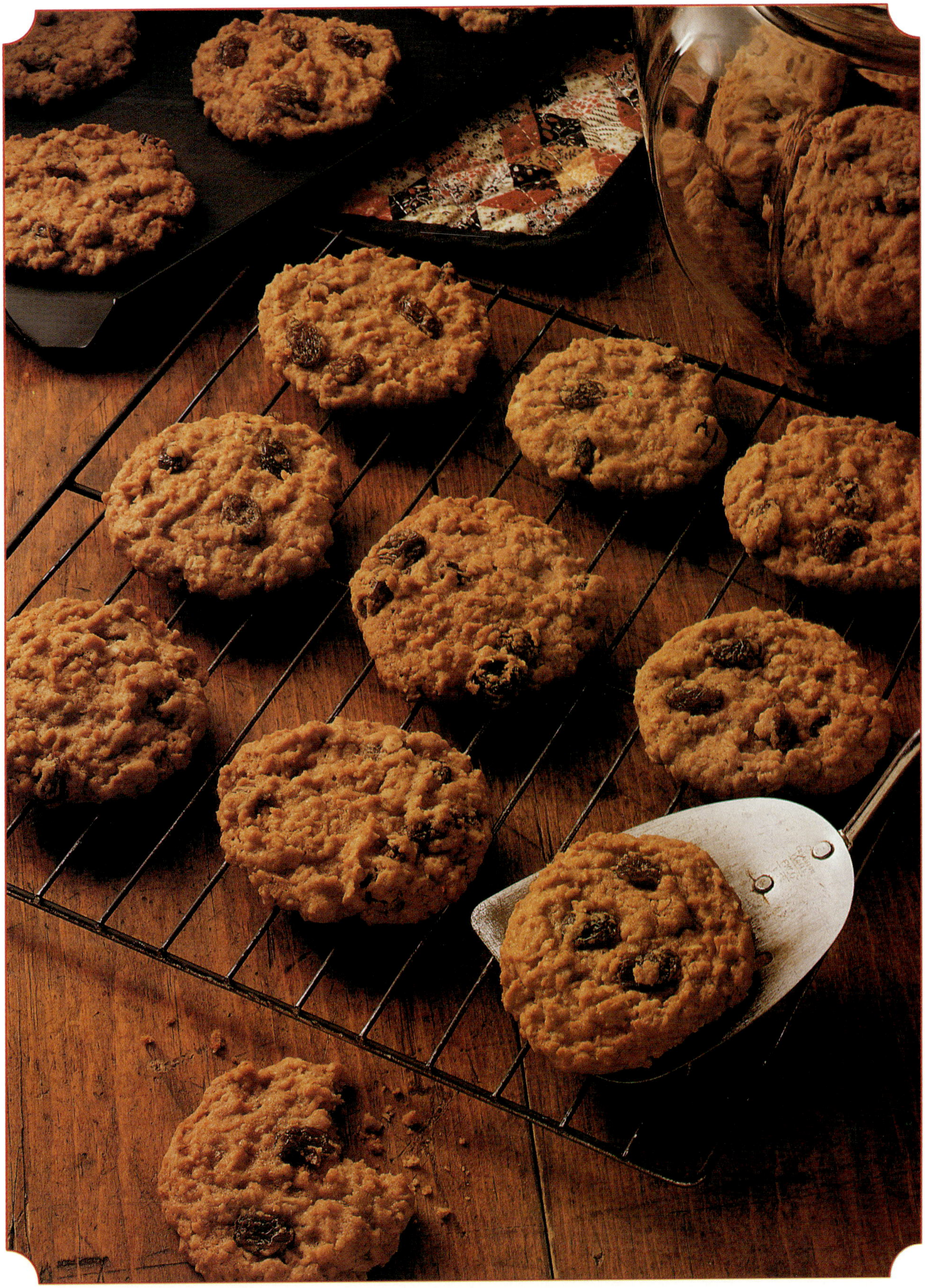

Lemon Doodles

Crisp on the outside and chewy on the inside—the lemon flavor adds a new twist to ever popular snickerdoodles.

Preparation time: 1 hour • Baking time: 7 minutes

2½ cups all-purpose flour
1½ cups sugar
¾ cup flaked coconut
1 cup LAND O LAKES® Butter, softened
2 eggs
1½ teaspoons cream of tartar
1 teaspoon baking soda
¼ teaspoon salt
½ teaspoon grated lemon peel
1 tablespoon lemon juice

Heat oven to 400°. In large mixer bowl combine all ingredients. Beat at low speed, scraping bowl often, until well mixed (2 to 4 minutes). Drop by rounded teaspoonfuls 2 inches apart onto cookie sheets. Bake for 7 to 10 minutes or until edges are lightly browned.
YIELD: 4 dozen cookies.

Nutrition Information (1 cookie): Calories 90; Protein 1g; Carbohydrate 12g; Fat 5g; Cholesterol 20mg; Sodium 75mg

Honey N' Spice Cookies

Orange, honey, nutmeg and cloves team up in these tender, soft drop cookies.

Preparation time: 1 hour • Baking time: 7 minutes

Cookies
- 2 cups all-purpose flour
- ¾ cup sugar
- ¾ cup LAND O LAKES® Butter, softened
- ¼ cup honey
- 1 egg
- ½ teaspoon salt
- ½ teaspoon baking soda
- ½ teaspoon nutmeg
- ¼ teaspoon cloves
- ½ teaspoon orange extract <u>or</u> vanilla

Glaze
- 1 cup powdered sugar
- 2 teaspoons grated orange peel
- 2 tablespoons milk

Heat oven to 375°. In large mixer bowl combine all cookie ingredients. Beat at low speed, scraping bowl often, until well mixed (1 to 2 minutes). Drop by rounded teaspoonfuls 2 inches apart onto cookie sheets. Bake for 7 to 10 minutes or until edges are lightly browned.

Meanwhile, in small bowl stir together all glaze ingredients. Frost warm cookies with glaze. **YIELD:** 3 dozen cookies.

Nutrition Information (1 cookie): Calories 100; Protein 1g; Carbohydrate 14g; Fat 4g; Cholesterol 15mg; Sodium 85mg

Jumbo Candy & Nut Cookies

These oversized cookies are a family favorite.

Preparation time: 45 minutes • Baking time: 13 minutes
(pictured on cover)

- 1 cup sugar
- 1 cup firmly packed brown sugar
- 1 cup LAND O LAKES® Butter, softened
- 2 eggs
- 1 tablespoon vanilla
- 2 cups all-purpose flour
- 1½ cups quick-cooking oats
- 1 teaspoon baking soda
- ½ teaspoon salt
- 1 (16-ounce) bag (2 cups) candy coated milk chocolate pieces
- 1 cup coarsely chopped peanuts

Heat oven to 350°. In large mixer bowl combine sugar, brown sugar, butter, eggs and vanilla. Beat at medium speed, scraping bowl often, until creamy (2 to 3 minutes). Reduce speed to low. Add all remaining ingredients <u>except</u> candy and peanuts. Continue beating, scraping bowl often, until well mixed (2 to 3 minutes). By hand, stir in candy and peanuts. Drop dough by scant ¼ cupfuls 2 inches apart onto greased cookie sheets. Bake for 13 to 16 minutes or until light golden brown. **YIELD:** 2 dozen cookies.

Nutrition Information (1 cookie): Calories 330; Protein 5g; Carbohydrate 41g; Fat 18g; Cholesterol 40mg; Sodium 200mg

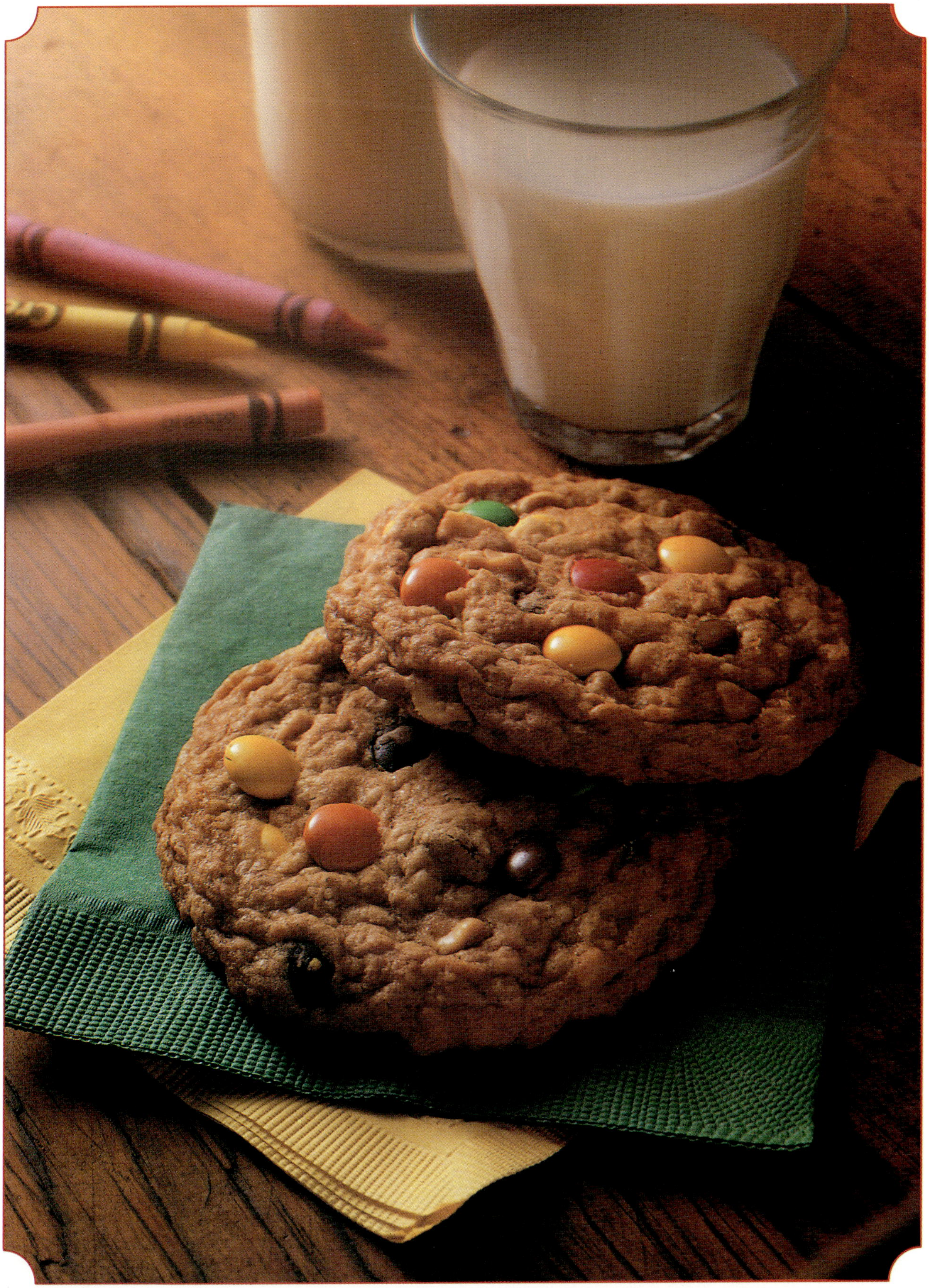

Nutty Chocolate Chunk Cookies

Everyone loves these buttery cookies chock full of chocolate and nuts.

Preparation time: 45 minutes • Baking time: 9 minutes

- ¾ cup firmly packed brown sugar
- ½ cup sugar
- 1 cup LAND O LAKES® Butter, softened
- 1 egg
- 1½ teaspoons vanilla
- 2¼ cups all-purpose flour
- 1 teaspoon baking soda
- ½ teaspoon salt
- 1 cup coarsely chopped walnuts
- 1 (8-ounce) bar milk chocolate, cut into ¼-inch pieces

Heat oven to 375°. In large mixer bowl combine brown sugar, sugar, butter, egg and vanilla. Beat at medium speed, scraping bowl often, until well mixed (1 to 2 minutes). Reduce speed to low; add flour, baking soda and salt. Continue beating, scraping bowl often, until well mixed (1 to 2 minutes). By hand, stir in walnuts and chocolate. Drop by rounded tablespoonfuls 2 inches apart onto cookie sheets. Bake for 9 to 11 minutes or until lightly browned. Let stand 1 minute; remove from cookie sheets. **YIELD:** 3 dozen cookies.

Nutrition Information (1 cookie): Calories 160; Protein 2g; Carbohydrate 17g; Fat 9g; Cholesterol 20mg; Sodium 120mg

Nutty Chocolate Chunk Cookies; Cookie Jar Cookies, see page 48

Cookie Jar Cookies

Coconut, oats and rice cereal will make these crisp and tender cookies a cookie jar favorite!

Preparation time: 1 hour • Baking time: 13 minutes
(pictured on page 47)

3 1/2	cups all-purpose flour
1	cup sugar
1	cup firmly packed brown sugar
2	cups LAND O LAKES® Butter, softened
1	egg
1	teaspoon baking soda
1/2	teaspoon salt
1	cup quick-cooking oats
1	cup crisp rice cereal
1	cup flaked coconut
1/2	cup chopped walnuts *or* pecans

Heat oven to 350°. In large mixer bowl combine all ingredients <u>except</u> oats, rice cereal, coconut and nuts. Beat at low speed, scraping bowl often, until well mixed (2 to 3 minutes). By hand, stir in all remaining ingredients. Drop by rounded tablespoonfuls 2 inches apart onto cookie sheets. Bake for 13 to 16 minutes or until lightly browned.

YIELD: 4 dozen cookies.

Nutrition Information (1 cookie): Calories 160; Protein 2g; Carbohydrate 18g; Fat 9g; Cholesterol 25mg; Sodium 135mg

Macadamia Nut White Chocolate Chunk Cookies

These crisp and chewy cookies are filled with white chocolate and macadamia nuts.

Preparation time: 45 minutes • Baking time: 9 minutes

- ¾ cup firmly packed brown sugar
- ½ cup LAND O LAKES® Butter, softened
- 1 egg
- 1½ teaspoons vanilla
- 1⅓ cups all-purpose flour
- ½ teaspoon baking powder
- ½ teaspoon baking soda
- ½ teaspoon salt
- 2 (3-ounce) bars white chocolate, cut into ½-inch pieces
- 1 (3½-ounce) jar (¾ cup) salted macadamia nuts, coarsely chopped

Heat oven to 350°. In large mixer bowl combine brown sugar, butter, egg and vanilla. Beat at medium speed, scraping bowl often, until well mixed (1 to 2 minutes). Reduce speed to low; add flour, baking powder, baking soda and salt. Continue beating, scraping bowl often, until well mixed (1 to 2 minutes). By hand, stir in white chocolate and macadamia nuts. Drop by rounded tablespoonfuls 2 inches apart onto greased cookie sheets. Bake for 9 to 12 minutes or until light golden brown. Cool 1 minute; remove from cookie sheets.

YIELD: 2 dozen cookies.

Nutrition Information (1 cookie): Calories 150; Protein 2g; Carbohydrate 17g; Fat 9g; Cholesterol 20mg; Sodium 120mg

Tart N' Tangy Lemonade Frosties

These cookies are reminiscent of a frosty glass of lemonade.

Preparation time: 1 hour 30 minutes • Baking time: 8 minutes • Cooling time: 15 minutes

Cookies
- 1¼ cups sugar
- 1¼ cups LAND O LAKES® Butter, softened
- 2 eggs
- 3 cups all-purpose flour
- 1 (6-ounce) can frozen lemonade <u>or</u> orange juice concentrate, thawed, <u>reserve 2 tablespoons for frosting</u>
- 1 teaspoon baking soda

Frosting
- 3 cups powdered sugar
- ⅓ cup LAND O LAKES® Butter, softened
- 2 tablespoons reserved frozen lemonade concentrate
- 1 teaspoon vanilla
- 1 to 2 tablespoons milk

- Yellow colored sugar, if desired

Heat oven to 400°. In large mixer bowl combine sugar, 1¼ cups butter and eggs. Beat at medium speed, scraping bowl often, until creamy (3 to 5 minutes). Reduce speed to low; continue beating, gradually adding flour, lemonade and baking soda and scraping bowl often, until well mixed (1 to 2 minutes). Drop by rounded teaspoonfuls onto cookie sheets. Bake for 8 to 14 minutes or until edges are lightly browned. Cool completely.

In small mixer bowl combine all frosting ingredients <u>except</u> milk and colored sugar. Beat at low speed, scraping bowl often and gradually adding enough milk for desired spreading consistency. Frost cooled cookies; sprinkle with colored sugar. **YIELD:** 4 dozen cookies.

Nutrition Information (1 cookie): Calories 140; Protein 1g; Carbohydrate 20g; Fat 6g; Cholesterol 25mg; Sodium 90mg

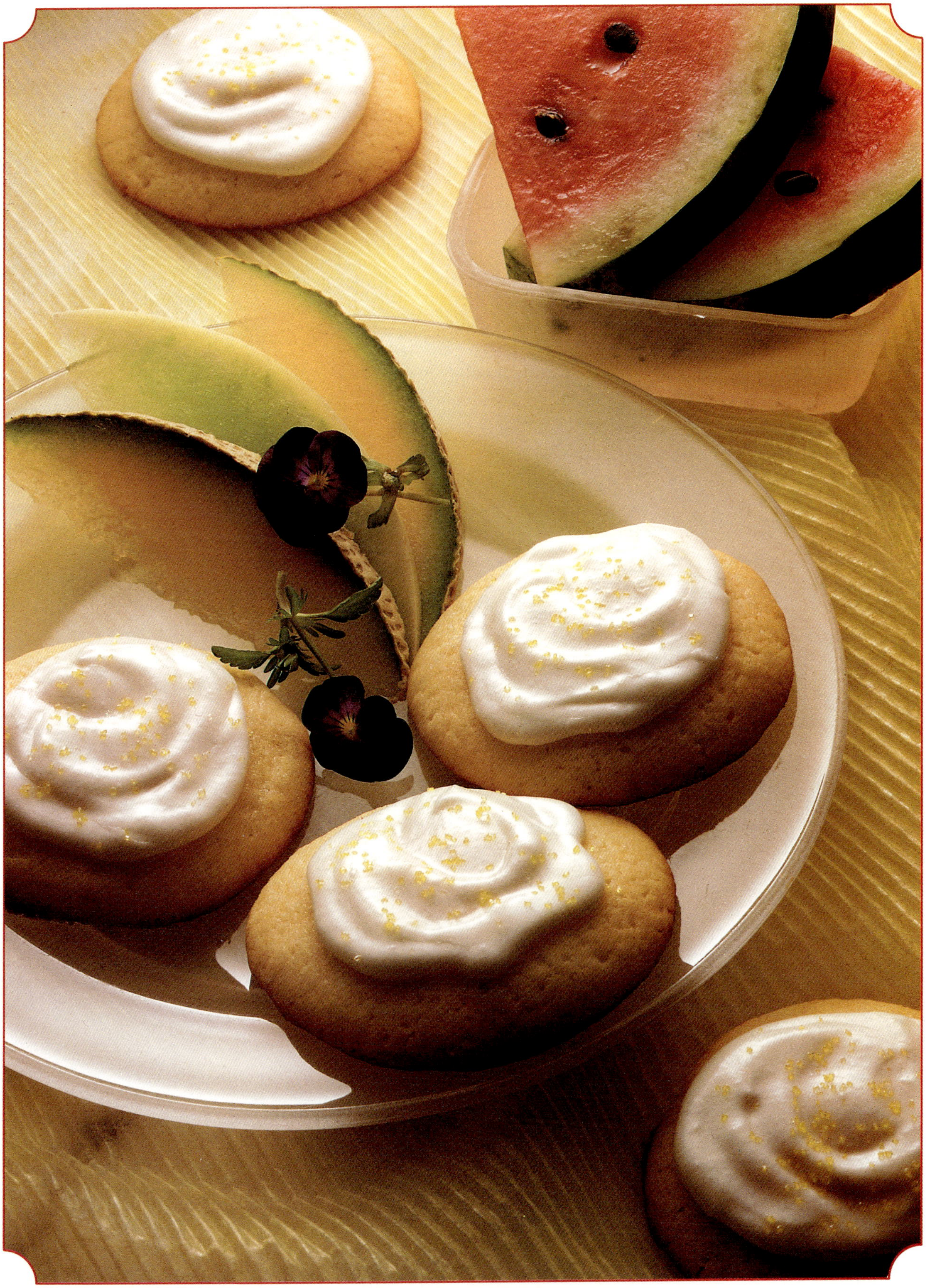

Versatile Butter Cookies

This is a traditional butter cookie with variations.

Preparation time: 1 hour • Baking time: 7 minutes

1 1/2 cups sugar
1 cup LAND O LAKES® Butter, softened
2 eggs
3 cups all-purpose flour
1 teaspoon baking soda
1 teaspoon vanilla

Heat oven to 400°. In large mixer bowl combine sugar, butter and eggs. Beat at medium speed, scraping bowl often, until creamy (3 to 5 minutes). Reduce speed to low; add all remaining ingredients. Continue beating, scraping bowl often, until well mixed (1 to 2 minutes). Divide dough in half; prepare desired variations using half of dough for each variation. Bake for 7 to 10 minutes or until edges are lightly browned. **YIELD:** 5 dozen cookies.

VARIATIONS

Cinnamon N' Sugar: Shape rounded teaspoonfuls of dough into 1-inch balls; dip in mixture of 2 tablespoons sugar and 2 teaspoons cinnamon. Place 2 inches apart on cookie sheets.

Cherry Chocolate Bits: By hand, stir in 1/4 cup chopped or grated semi-sweet chocolate. Shape rounded teaspoonfuls of dough into 1-inch balls. Place 2 inches apart on cookie sheets. Press 1 drained maraschino cherry half into center of each ball.

Coconut Balls: By hand, stir in 1/2 cup flaked coconut. Shape rounded teaspoonfuls of dough into 1-inch balls. Place 2 inches apart on cookie sheets. After baking, roll in powdered sugar to coat.

Spice or Nut Drops: Shape rounded teaspoonfuls of dough into 1-inch balls. Place 2 inches apart on cookie sheets. Press 1 spice gumdrop or whole blanched almond into center of each ball.

Nutrition Information (1 cookie): Calories 70; Protein 1g; Carbohydrate 10g; Fat 3g; Cholesterol 15mg; Sodium 50mg

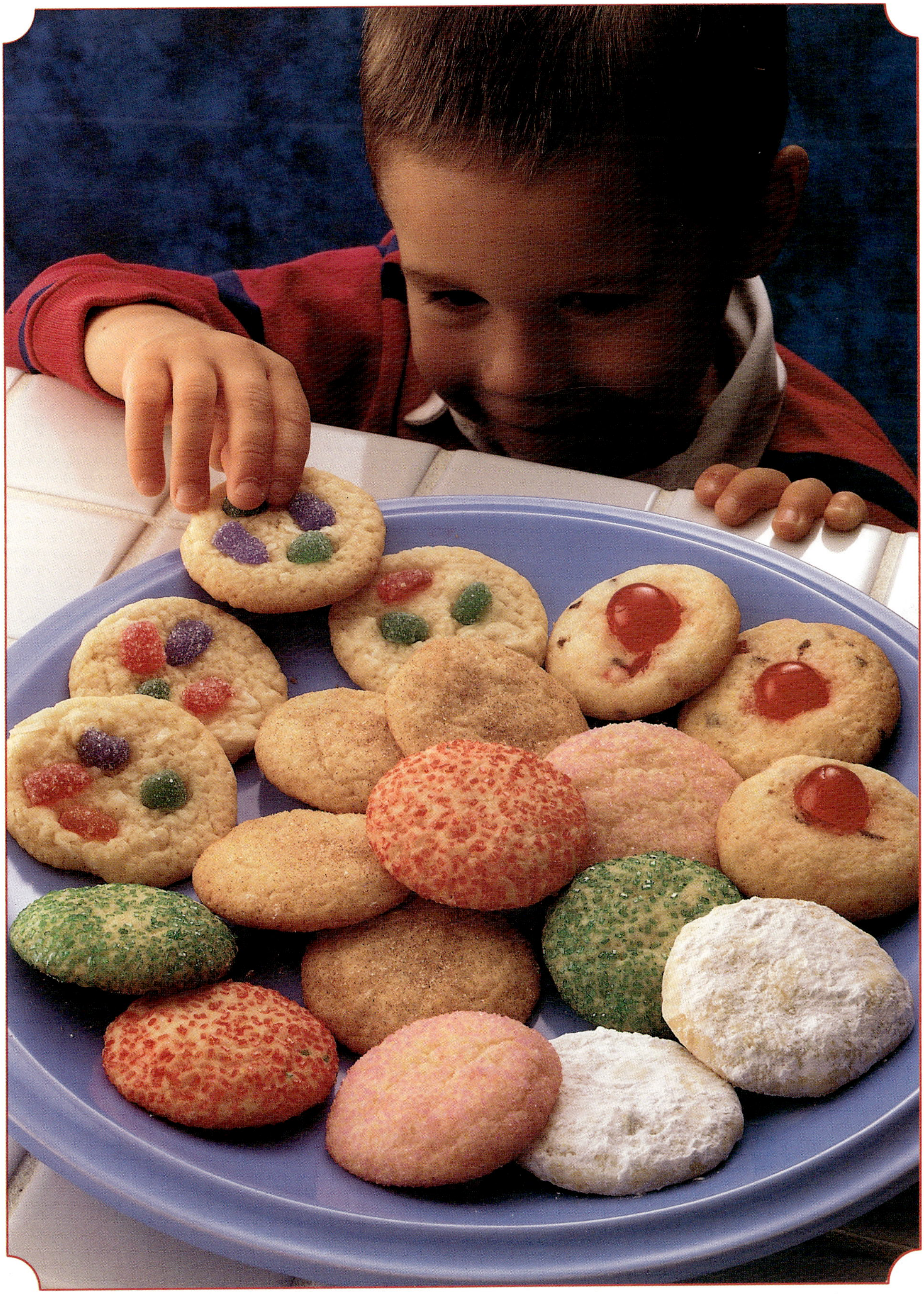

Bars

～

When you're asked to bring a plate of bars to the next school function or pot-luck supper, turn to this chapter for inspiration. Caramel Rocky Road Bars are always a favorite. Grasshopper Butter Cream Bars and Old-World Raspberry Bars will add a special touch to any occasion.

Frosted Orange Date Bars, see page 57; Cheesecake Squares, see page 56

Cheesecake Squares

The flavor of cheesecake in an easy-to-make bar.

Preparation time: 30 minutes • Baking time: 31 minutes
(pictured on page 55)

Crust
- 1 cup all-purpose flour
- 1/2 cup firmly packed brown sugar
- 1/3 cup LAND O LAKES® Butter, softened
- 1/2 cup chopped walnuts or pecans

Filling
- 1 (8-ounce) package cream cheese, softened
- 1/4 cup sugar
- 1 egg
- 2 tablespoons lemon juice
- 2 tablespoons milk
- 1/2 teaspoon vanilla

Heat oven to 350°. In large mixer bowl combine flour, brown sugar and butter. Beat at low speed, scraping bowl often, until mixture is crumbly (2 to 3 minutes). By hand, stir in walnuts. Reserve 1 cup mixture for topping; press remaining mixture on bottom of 8-inch square baking pan. Bake for 8 to 10 minutes or until lightly browned.

Meanwhile, in small mixer bowl combine all filling ingredients. Beat at medium speed, scraping bowl often, until smooth (4 to 5 minutes). Spread over hot partially baked crust. Sprinkle with reserved crumb mixture. Continue baking for 23 to 30 minutes or until golden brown. Cool completely; cut into bars. Store refrigerated. **YIELD:** 25 bars.

VARIATION

Holiday Squares: Stir 1/4 cup chopped red candied cherries and 1/4 cup chopped green candied cherries into filling mixture.

Nutrition Information (1 bar): Calories 120; Protein 2g; Carbohydrate 11g; Fat 7g; Cholesterol 25mg; Sodium 60mg

Frosted Orange Date Bars

Luxuriously moist, old-fashioned date bars are accented with orange peel and a buttery orange frosting.

Preparation time: 1 hour 15 minutes • Baking time: 15 minutes • Cooling time: 30 minutes
(pictured on page 55)

Bars
- 3/4 cup sugar
- 1/2 cup LAND O LAKES® Butter
- 1/2 cup water
- 1 (8-ounce) package chopped dates
- 1 1/4 cups all-purpose flour
- 1 cup chopped pecans
- 3/4 cup milk
- 1/4 cup orange juice
- 2 eggs
- 3/4 teaspoon baking soda
- 1/2 teaspoon salt
- 1 tablespoon grated orange peel

Frosting
- 3 cups powdered sugar
- 1/3 cup LAND O LAKES® Butter, softened
- 1 (3-ounce) package cream cheese, softened
- 1 tablespoon grated orange peel
- 2 to 3 tablespoons orange juice

Heat oven to 350°. In 3-quart saucepan combine sugar, 1/2 cup butter, water and dates. Cook over low heat, stirring constantly, until dates are softened (5 to 8 minutes). Remove from heat. By hand, stir in all remaining bar ingredients until well mixed. Spread into greased 15x10x1-inch jelly roll pan. Bake for 15 to 20 minutes or until toothpick inserted in center comes out clean. Cool completely.

In small mixer bowl combine all frosting ingredients <u>except</u> orange juice. Beat at medium speed, scraping bowl often and adding enough orange juice for desired spreading consistency. Frost cooled bars; cut into bars. **YIELD: 48 bars.**

Nutrition Information (1 bar): Calories 120; Protein 1g; Carbohydrate 16g; Fat 6g; Cholesterol 20mg; Sodium 85mg

Caramel N' Chocolate Pecan Bars

Popular candy flavors combined in an easy bar.

Preparation time: 30 minutes • Baking time: 18 minutes

Crust
- 2 cups all-purpose flour
- 1 cup firmly packed brown sugar
- ½ cup LAND O LAKES® Butter, softened

- 1 cup pecan halves

Caramel Layer
- ⅔ cup LAND O LAKES® Butter
- ½ cup firmly packed brown sugar

- 1 (6-ounce) package (1 cup) semi-sweet real chocolate chips

Heat oven to 350°. In large mixer bowl combine all crust ingredients except pecans. Beat at medium speed, scraping bowl often, until well mixed and particles are fine (2 to 3 minutes). Press on bottom of 13x9-inch baking pan. Sprinkle pecans evenly over unbaked crust.

In 1-quart saucepan combine ⅔ cup butter and ½ cup brown sugar. Cook over medium heat, stirring constantly, until mixture comes to a full boil. Boil, stirring constantly, until candy thermometer reaches 242°F or small amount of mixture dropped into ice water forms a firm ball (about 1 minute). Pour evenly over pecans and crust. Bake for 18 to 22 minutes or until entire caramel layer is bubbly. Remove from oven. Sprinkle with chocolate chips; let stand 2 to 3 minutes. With knife, swirl chips leaving some whole for marbled effect. Cool completely; cut into bars. **YIELD:** 36 bars.

Nutrition Information (1 bar): Calories 160; Protein 1g; Carbohydrate 18g; Fat 10g; Cholesterol 15mg; Sodium 65mg

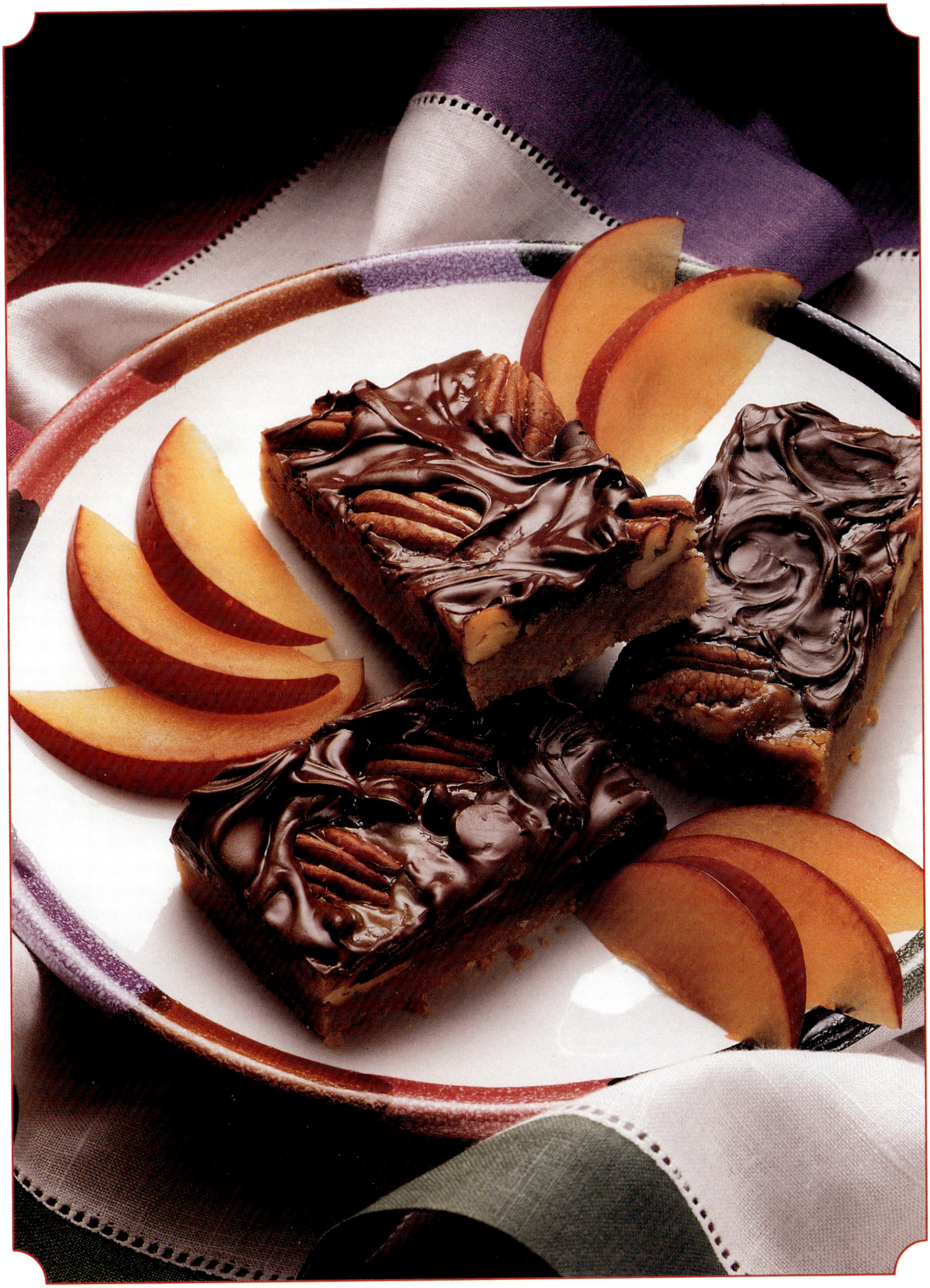

Caramel Chew Coconut Bars

Caramel and coconut blend together for a deliciously rich bar that's accented with a touch of orange.

Preparation time: 45 minutes • Baking time: 32 minutes

Crumb Mixture
- 2 cups all-purpose flour
- ½ cup sugar
- ¾ cup LAND O LAKES® Butter, softened

Filling
- ¾ cup firmly packed brown sugar
- 2 eggs
- 2 tablespoons all-purpose flour
- ½ teaspoon baking powder
- ½ teaspoon salt
- 1 teaspoon vanilla
- 1½ cups flaked coconut
- 1 cup chopped pecans

Glaze
- 1½ cups powdered sugar
- ¼ cup orange juice
- 1 tablespoon grated orange peel

Heat oven to 350°. In small mixer bowl combine all crumb mixture ingredients. Beat at low speed, scraping bowl often, until well mixed and particles are fine (2 to 3 minutes). Press on bottom of 13x9-inch baking pan. Bake for 15 to 20 minutes or until edges are very lightly browned.

Meanwhile, in same small mixer bowl combine all filling ingredients <u>except</u> coconut and pecans. Beat at medium speed, scraping bowl often, until well mixed (1 to 2 minutes). By hand, stir in coconut and pecans. Pour filling over hot partially baked crust. Continue baking for 17 to 20 minutes or until toothpick inserted in center comes out clean.

In small bowl stir together all glaze ingredients. Drizzle glaze over warm bars. Cool completely; cut into bars. **YIELD:** 36 bars.

Nutrition Information (1 bar): Calories 150; Protein 2g; Carbohydrate 19g; Fat 7g; Cholesterol 20mg; Sodium 80mg

Cherry Almond Chocolate Bars

A buttery pat-in-the-pan crust is topped with cherry preserves and almonds and then drizzled with a chocolate glaze for a very attractive and delicious bar cookie!

Preparation time: 30 minutes • Baking time: 20 minutes

Crumb Mixture
- 2 cups all-purpose flour
- 1/2 cup sugar
- 3/4 cup LAND O LAKES® Butter, softened

Filling
- 1 cup cherry preserves
- 1 (2 1/2-ounce) package (2/3 cup) sliced almonds
- 1/2 teaspoon almond extract

Glaze
- 1/3 cup milk <u>or</u> semi-sweet real chocolate chips
- 1 tablespoon LAND O LAKES® Butter
- 1/3 cup powdered sugar
- 1 tablespoon milk
- 1/2 teaspoon vanilla

Heat oven to 350°. In large mixer bowl combine all crumb mixture ingredients. Beat at low speed, scraping bowl often, until well mixed (2 to 3 minutes). Press crumb mixture on bottom of 13x9-inch baking pan. Bake for 20 to 25 minutes or until edges are lightly browned.

In same mixer bowl stir together all filling ingredients. Spread filling over hot crust.

In 1-quart saucepan melt chocolate chips and 1 tablespoon butter over low heat, stirring occasionally, until smooth (2 to 3 minutes). Stir in all remaining glaze ingredients. Drizzle warm glaze over bars. Cool completely; cut into bars. **YIELD:** 36 bars.

Nutrition Information (1 bar): Calories 120; Protein 1g; Carbohydrate 16g; Fat 6g; Cholesterol 10mg; Sodium 45mg

Caramel Rocky Road Bars

*Caramel, peanut, marshmallow and chocolate lovers,
BEWARE—these bars may be deliciously habit-forming!*

Preparation time: 30 minutes • Baking time: 32 minutes • Chilling time: 1 hour

Crumb Mixture
- 1 cup all-purpose flour
- ¾ cup quick-cooking oats
- ½ cup sugar
- ½ cup LAND O LAKES® Butter, softened
- ½ teaspoon baking soda
- ¼ teaspoon salt
- ¼ cup chopped salted peanuts

Filling
- ½ cup caramel ice cream topping
- ½ cup salted peanuts
- 1½ cups miniature marshmallows
- ½ cup milk chocolate chips

Heat oven to 350°. In small mixer bowl combine all crumb mixture ingredients <u>except</u> chopped peanuts. Beat at low speed, scraping bowl often, until mixture is crumbly (1 to 2 minutes). By hand, stir in ¼ cup peanuts. <u>Reserve ¾ cup crumb mixture</u>; set aside. Press remaining crumb mixture on bottom of greased and floured 9-inch square baking pan. Bake for 12 to 17 minutes or until lightly browned.

Spread caramel topping evenly over hot partially baked crust. Sprinkle with ½ cup peanuts, marshmallows and chocolate chips. Crumble reserved crumb mixture over chocolate chips. Continue baking for 20 to 25 minutes or until crumb mixture is lightly browned. Refrigerate until firm (at least 1 hour). Cut into bars. **YIELD:** 25 bars.

Nutrition Information (1 bar): Calories 120; Protein 2g; Carbohydrate 16g; Fat 6g; Cholesterol 10mg; Sodium 120mg

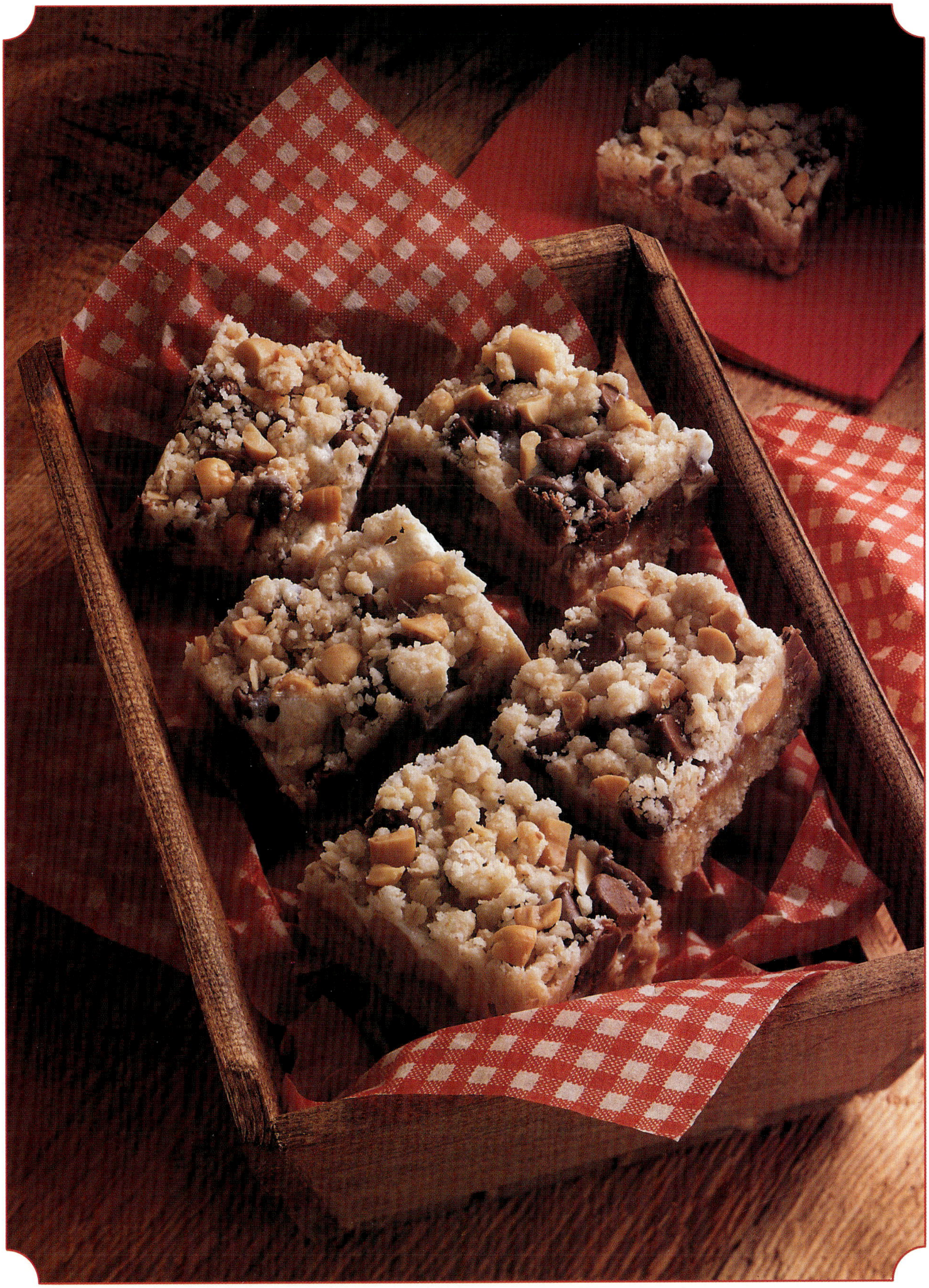

Chocolate Caramel Oatmeal Bars

These chewy caramel bars are utterly delicious.

Preparation time: 45 minutes • Baking time: 28 minutes • Cooling time: 1 hour

Crumb Mixture
- 1½ cups all-purpose flour
- 1 cup quick-cooking oats
- 1 cup firmly packed brown sugar
- ¾ cup LAND O LAKES® Butter, softened
- ¾ teaspoon baking soda
- ½ teaspoon salt

Caramel Mixture
- ½ cup milk
- 1 (14-ounce) package (48) caramels, unwrapped

Filling
- 1 cup semi-sweet real chocolate chips
- ½ cup chopped pecans

Topping
- 1 cup semi-sweet real chocolate chips, melted
- 60 (about 5 ounces) pecan halves

Heat oven to 350°. In large mixer bowl combine all crumb mixture ingredients. Beat at medium speed, scraping bowl often, until mixture is crumbly (2 to 3 minutes). Reserve 1 cup crumb mixture; set aside. Press remaining mixture on bottom of 13x9-inch baking pan. Bake for 10 minutes.

Meanwhile, in 2-quart saucepan combine milk and caramels. Cook over medium low heat, stirring occasionally, until caramels melt and mixture is creamy (15 to 20 minutes). Sprinkle hot partially baked crust with 1 cup chocolate chips and ½ cup chopped pecans. Pour caramel mixture evenly over chocolate chips and pecans. Sprinkle with reserved crumb mixture; pat lightly. Bake for 18 to 22 minutes or until caramel is bubbly around edges. Cool completely; cut into bars.

On each bar, place ½ teaspoon melted chocolate; top with pecan half. Store in tightly covered container. **YIELD:** 60 bars.

Nutrition Information (1 bar): Calories 130; Protein 1g; Carbohydrate 16g; Fat 7g; Cholesterol 5mg; Sodium 70mg

Chocolate Meringue Peanut Bars

These bars are topped with a meringue that has peanuts and chocolate chips.

Preparation time: 30 minutes • Baking time: 30 minutes

Crumb Mixture
- 1½ cups all-purpose flour
- ½ cup sugar
- ¾ cup LAND O LAKES® Butter, softened
- 2 eggs, separated, <u>reserve whites</u>
- 2 teaspoons vanilla

Filling
- 2 reserved egg whites
- ⅓ cup sugar
- 1 cup chopped salted peanuts
- ½ cup milk chocolate chips

Heat oven to 325°. In large mixer bowl combine all crumb mixture ingredients. Beat at low speed, scraping bowl often, until crumbly (1 to 2 minutes). Press on bottom of greased 13x9-inch pan; set aside.

In small mixer bowl beat egg whites at high speed, scraping bowl often, until soft peaks form (1 to 2 minutes). Continue beating, gradually adding sugar, until stiff peaks form (1 to 2 minutes). By hand, gently stir in peanuts and chocolate chips. Spread over crumb mixture. Bake for 30 to 35 minutes or until lightly browned. Cool completely; cut into bars. **YIELD: 36 bars.**

Nutrition Information (1 bar): Calories 110; Protein 2g; Carbohydrate 11g; Fat 7g; Cholesterol 25mg; Sodium 80mg

Grasshopper Butter Cream Bars

A combination of mint and chocolate makes this butter cream frosted bar taste like a grasshopper pie.

Preparation time: 30 minutes • Baking time: 15 minutes • Cooling time: 20 minutes • Chilling time: 1 hour

Crust
- 3/4 cup sugar
- 3/4 cup LAND O LAKES® Butter, softened
- 1 tablespoon whipping cream or milk
- 1 1/2 cups all-purpose flour
- 1/2 cup chopped hazelnuts, filberts or walnuts
- 1/2 teaspoon baking powder
- 1/2 teaspoon crème de menthe flavoring*
- 1 (6-ounce) package (1 cup) semi-sweet real chocolate chips

Topping
- 4 cups powdered sugar
- 1/4 cup LAND O LAKES® Butter, softened
- 1 (3-ounce) package cream cheese, softened
- 1/2 teaspoon salt
- 1/2 teaspoon crème de menthe flavoring*
- 3 to 4 tablespoons whipping cream or milk

Heat oven to 350°. In small mixer bowl combine sugar, 3/4 cup butter and 1 tablespoon cream. Beat at medium speed, scraping bowl often, until creamy (1 minute). By hand, stir in all remaining crust ingredients except chocolate chips. Press on bottom of 13x9-inch baking pan. Bake for 15 to 20 minutes or until edges are lightly browned. Sprinkle with chocolate chips. Let stand 2 minutes; spread chips over crust. Cool 20 minutes.

Meanwhile, in large mixer bowl combine powdered sugar, 1/4 cup butter, cream cheese, salt and 1/2 teaspoon crème de menthe flavoring. Beat at medium speed, scraping bowl often and gradually adding enough whipping cream for desired spreading consistency. Spread over cooled chocolate layer. Cover; refrigerate until firm (at least 1 hour). Cut into bars. Store refrigerated. **YIELD:** 48 bars.

* 1/2 teaspoon peppermint extract can be substituted for 1/2 teaspoon crème de menthe flavoring.

Nutrition Information (1 bar): Calories 130; Protein 1g; Carbohydrate 17g; Fat 7g; Cholesterol 15mg; Sodium 70mg

Grasshopper Butter Cream Bars; Old-World Raspberry Bars, see page 68

Old-World Raspberry Bars

Rich, moist bars filled with flavorful raspberry preserves.

Preparation time: 15 minutes • Baking time: 40 minutes
(pictured on page 67)

2¼ cups all-purpose flour
1 cup sugar
1 cup chopped pecans
1 cup LAND O LAKES® Butter, softened
1 egg
1 (10-ounce) jar (¾ cup) raspberry preserves*

Heat oven to 350°. In large mixer bowl combine all ingredients <u>except</u> raspberry preserves. Beat at low speed, scraping bowl often, until well mixed (2 to 3 minutes). <u>Reserve 1½ cups mixture</u>; set aside. Press remaining mixture on bottom of greased 8-inch square baking pan. Spread preserves to within ½ inch of edge. Crumble reserved mixture over preserves. Bake for 40 to 50 minutes or until lightly browned. Cool completely; cut into bars. **YIELD:** 25 bars.

*1 (10-ounce) jar your favorite flavor preserves can be substituted for 1 (10-ounce) jar raspberry preserves.

Nutrition Information (1 bar): Calories 210; Protein 2g; Carbohydrate 27g; Fat 11g; Cholesterol 30mg; Sodium 85mg

Graham Cracker Caramel Crisps

Graham crackers are topped with marshmallows, buttery syrup and lots of almonds and coconut.

Preparation time: 30 minutes • Baking time: 8 minutes

- 12 double (5x2½-inch) graham crackers
- 2 cups miniature marshmallows
- ¾ cup firmly packed brown sugar
- ¾ cup LAND O LAKES® Butter
- 1 teaspoon cinnamon
- 1 teaspoon vanilla
- 1 cup sliced almonds
- 1 cup flaked coconut

Heat oven to 350°. Line 15x10x1-inch jelly roll pan with graham crackers; sprinkle evenly with marshmallows. In 2-quart saucepan combine brown sugar, butter, cinnamon and vanilla. Cook over medium heat, stirring occasionally, until mixture comes to a full boil (3 to 5 minutes). Boil, stirring constantly, 5 minutes. Immediately pour evenly over marshmallows; sprinkle with almonds and coconut. Bake for 8 to 12 minutes or until lightly browned. Cool completely; cut into bars. **YIELD:** 48 bars.

Nutrition Information (1 bar): Calories 80; Protein 1g; Carbohydrate 9g; Fat 5g; Cholesterol 10mg; Sodium 55mg

Lemon-Butter Bars

Tangy lemon and creamy butter combine to make these classic bars.

Preparation time: 30 minutes • Baking time: 33 minutes

Crust
1 1/3 cups all-purpose flour
1/4 cup sugar
1/2 cup LAND O LAKES® Butter, softened

Filling
3/4 cup sugar
2 eggs
2 tablespoons all-purpose flour
1/4 teaspoon baking powder
3 tablespoons lemon juice

Powdered sugar

Heat oven to 350°. In small mixer bowl combine all crust ingredients. Beat at low speed, scraping bowl often, until mixture is crumbly (2 to 3 minutes). Press on bottom of 8-inch square baking pan. Bake for 15 to 20 minutes or until edges are lightly browned.

Meanwhile, in small mixer bowl combine all filling ingredients <u>except</u> powdered sugar. Beat at low speed, scraping bowl often, until well mixed. Pour filling over hot partially baked crust. Continue baking for 18 to 20 minutes or until filling is set. Sprinkle with powdered sugar while still warm and again when cool. Cut into bars. **YIELD:** 16 bars.

Nutrition Information (1 bar): Calories 150; Protein 2g; Carbohydrate 22g; Fat 6g; Cholesterol 40mg; Sodium 70mg

Lemon-Butter Bars; Strawberry Marzipan Bars, see page 72

Strawberry Marzipan Bars

These European-inspired bars have a very special flavor and texture that makes them rich and extra elegant!

Preparation time: 30 minutes • Baking time: 35 minutes • Cooling time: 30 minutes
(pictured on page 71)

Crumb Mixture
- 1¼ cups all-purpose flour
- ⅓ cup firmly packed brown sugar
- ½ cup LAND O LAKES® Butter, softened

Filling
- ¾ cup strawberry preserves
- ½ cup all-purpose flour
- ½ cup firmly packed brown sugar
- ¼ cup LAND O LAKES® Butter, softened
- ½ teaspoon almond extract

Glaze
- ½ cup powdered sugar
- ½ teaspoon almond extract
- 1 to 2 teaspoons milk

Heat oven to 350°. In small mixer bowl combine all crumb mixture ingredients. Beat at low speed, scraping bowl often, until mixture is crumbly (1 to 2 minutes). Press on bottom of greased and floured 9-inch square baking pan. Bake for 15 to 20 minutes or until edges are lightly browned.

Spread preserves to within ¼ inch of edge. In same mixer bowl combine all remaining filling ingredients. Beat at low speed, scraping bowl often, until well mixed (1 to 2 minutes). Sprinkle filling ingredients over preserves. Continue baking for 20 to 25 minutes or until edges are lightly browned. Cool completely.

In small bowl stir together powdered sugar and ½ teaspoon almond extract. Gradually stir in enough milk for desired drizzling consistency. Drizzle over cooled bars; cut into bars. **YIELD:** 36 bars.

Nutrition Information (1 bar): Calories 100; Protein 1g; Carbohydrate 15g; Fat 4g; Cholesterol 10mg; Sodium 40mg

Lemon Coconut Bars

A tart, refreshing lemon flavor is accented with the sweetness of coconut in these rich butter bars.

Preparation time: 30 minutes • Baking time: 35 minutes

Crust
- 1½ cups all-purpose flour
- ¼ cup sugar
- ½ cup LAND O LAKES® Butter, softened
- 2 teaspoons grated lemon peel

Filling
- ¾ cup sugar
- ½ cup flaked coconut
- ¼ cup LAND O LAKES® Butter, softened
- 2 eggs
- ¼ cup lemon juice
- 2 teaspoons grated lemon peel

Heat oven to 350°. In small mixer bowl combine all crust ingredients. Beat at low speed, scraping bowl often, until crumbly (1 to 2 minutes). Press on bottom of 9-inch square baking pan. Bake for 15 to 20 minutes or until edges are lightly browned.

Meanwhile, in same mixer bowl combine all filling ingredients. Beat at low speed until well mixed (1 to 2 minutes). Pour over hot partially baked crust. Continue baking for 20 to 30 minutes or until filling is lightly browned and set. Cool completely; cut into bars.
YIELD: 25 bars.

Nutrition Information (1 bar): Calories 130; Protein 1g; Carbohydrate 15g; Fat 7g; Cholesterol 35mg; Sodium 65mg

Peanut Brittle Bars

These bars are reminiscent of an old-fashioned candy.

Preparation time: 30 minutes • Baking time: 15 minutes • Cooling time: 30 minutes

Bars
- 1 cup sugar
- 1 cup LAND O LAKES® Butter, softened
- ½ teaspoon salt
- 1 teaspoon vanilla
- 2 cups all-purpose flour
- 1 cup salted peanuts <u>or</u> chopped salted cashews
- 1 (6-ounce) package (1 cup) semi-sweet real chocolate chips

Glaze
- 1 cup powdered sugar
- 2 tablespoons creamy peanut butter
- 2 to 3 tablespoons hot water

Heat oven to 375°. In large mixer bowl combine sugar, butter, salt and vanilla. Beat at medium speed, scraping bowl often, until creamy (2 to 3 minutes). Reduce speed to low; add flour. Continue beating until well mixed (2 to 3 minutes). (Mixture will form clumps.) By hand, stir in peanuts and chocolate chips. Press on bottom of 15x10x1-inch jelly roll pan. Bake for 15 to 25 minutes or until edges are golden brown. Cool completely.

In medium bowl stir together powdered sugar and peanut butter. Gradually stir in enough hot water for desired glazing consistency. Drizzle glaze over bars. Cut into bars or break into irregular pieces. **YIELD:** 48 bars.

VARIATION

<u>Almond Bark</u>: <u>Omit peanuts and chocolate chips</u>. <u>Omit peanut butter in glaze</u>. Prepare bars using 1 cup sliced almonds and 1 cup milk chocolate chips. Prepare glaze using 2 tablespoons softened LAND O LAKES® Butter and ½ teaspoon almond extract.

Nutrition Information (1 bar): Calories 120; Protein 2g; Carbohydrate 13g; Fat 7g; Cholesterol 10mg; Sodium 90mg

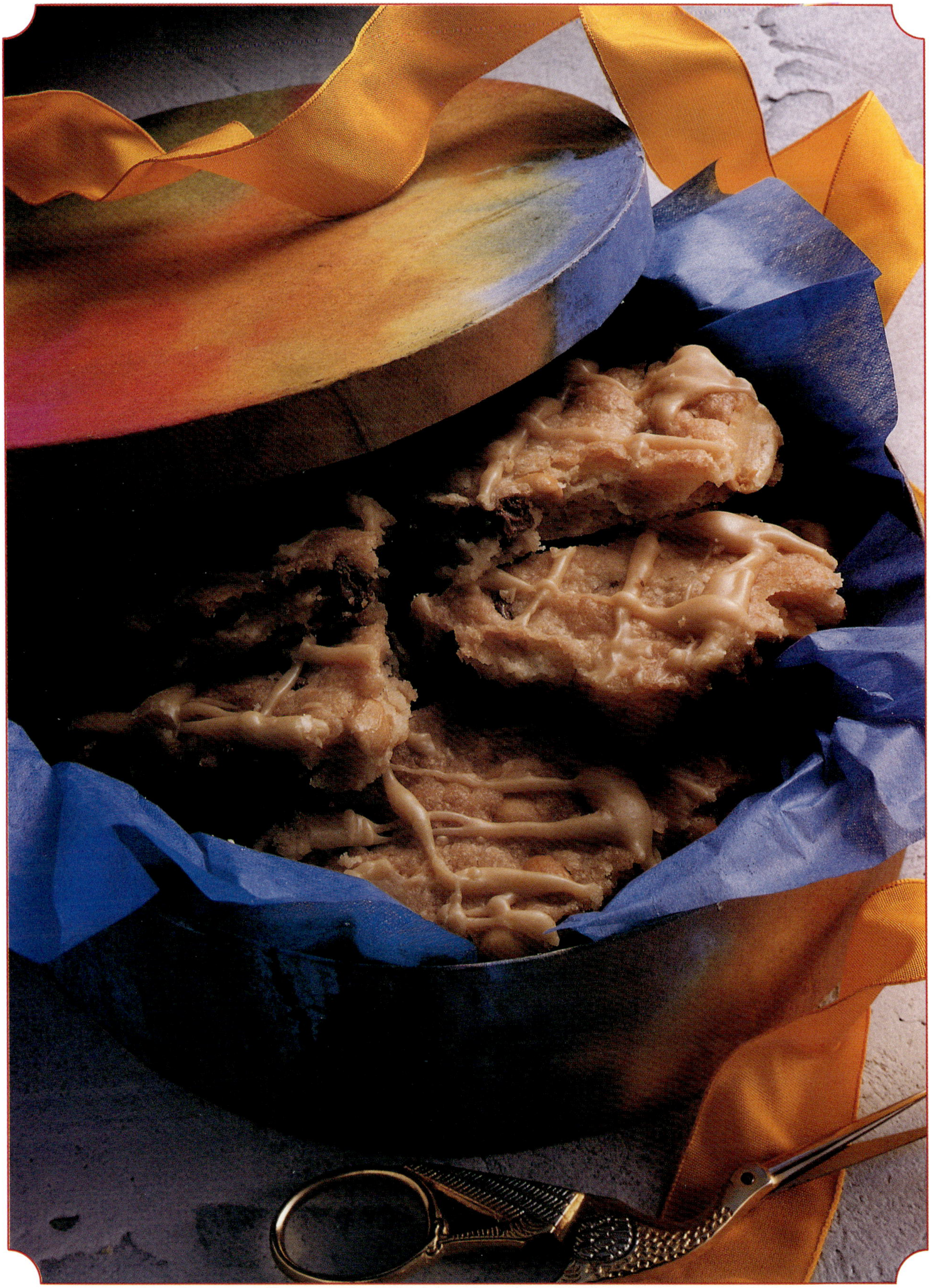

English Toffee Bars

Milk chocolate swirls atop a cinnamon-flavored crust to create a tempting bar cookie.

Preparation time: 30 minutes • Baking time: 40 minutes

- 1 cup sugar
- 1 cup LAND O LAKES® Butter, softened
- 1 egg, separated
- 1¾ cups all-purpose flour
- 1 teaspoon cinnamon
- 1 cup chopped pecans
- 1 cup milk <u>or</u> semi-sweet real chocolate chips

Heat oven to 275°. In small mixer bowl beat sugar and butter at medium speed, scraping bowl often, until well mixed (1 to 2 minutes). Add egg yolk; continue beating until well mixed. Reduce speed to low. Continue beating, gradually adding flour and cinnamon and scraping bowl often, until well mixed (1 to 2 minutes). Press evenly on bottom of 15x10x1-inch jelly roll pan.

In small bowl, with fork, beat egg white; brush over top of dough. Sprinkle with pecans; pat lightly into dough. Bake for 40 to 50 minutes or until edges are lightly browned.

Sprinkle with chocolate chips; let stand 3 minutes. With knife, swirl chips slightly. Cut while warm into squares, triangles or diamonds. Cool in pan on wire cooling rack. **YIELD:** 48 bars.

Nutrition Information (1 bar): Calories 100; Protein 1g; Carbohydrate 10g; Fat 7g; Cholesterol 15mg; Sodium 45mg

Mocha Almond Bars

Coffee and almonds give this bar a unique flavor and a crunchy texture.

Preparation time: 30 minutes • Baking time: 25 minutes

Bars
- 2¼ cups all-purpose flour
- 1 cup sugar
- 1 cup LAND O LAKES® Butter, softened
- 1 egg
- 1 teaspoon instant coffee granules
- 1 cup sliced almonds

Glaze
- ¾ cup powdered sugar
- 1 to 2 tablespoons milk
- ¼ teaspoon almond extract

Heat oven to 350°. In small mixer bowl combine all bar ingredients <u>except</u> almonds. Beat at low speed, scraping bowl often, until well mixed (2 to 3 minutes). By hand, stir in almonds. Press on bottom of greased 13x9-inch baking pan. Bake for 25 to 30 minutes or until edges are lightly browned.

Meanwhile, in small bowl stir together all glaze ingredients. Drizzle glaze over warm bars. Cool completely; cut into bars. **YIELD:** 36 bars.

Nutrition Information (1 bar): Calories 120; Protein 2g; Carbohydrate 14g; Fat 7g; Cholesterol 20mg; Sodium 55mg

Peanut Butter Chocolate Bars

These bars are "heavenly" good.

Preparation time: 30 minutes • Baking time: 32 minutes

Crust
- 1 cup all-purpose flour
- ⅓ cup sugar
- ½ cup LAND O LAKES® Butter, softened

Filling
- ½ cup sugar
- ¼ cup crunchy-style peanut butter
- ½ cup light corn syrup
- 2 eggs
- ¼ teaspoon salt
- ½ teaspoon vanilla
- ½ cup semi-sweet chocolate chips
- ½ cup flaked coconut

Heat oven to 350°. In small mixer bowl combine all crust ingredients. Beat at low speed, scraping bowl often, until mixture is crumbly (1 to 2 minutes). Press on bottom of greased 9-inch square baking pan. Bake for 12 to 17 minutes or until edges are lightly browned.

Meanwhile, in same mixer bowl combine all filling ingredients except chocolate chips and coconut. Beat at low speed, scraping bowl often, until well mixed (1 to 2 minutes). By hand, stir in chocolate chips and coconut; pour over hot partially baked crust. Continue baking for 20 to 30 minutes or until filling is set and golden brown. Cool completely; cut into bars. **YIELD:** 25 bars.

Nutrition Information (1 bar): Calories 140; Protein 2g; Carbohydrate 19g; Fat 7g; Cholesterol 27mg; Sodium 82mg

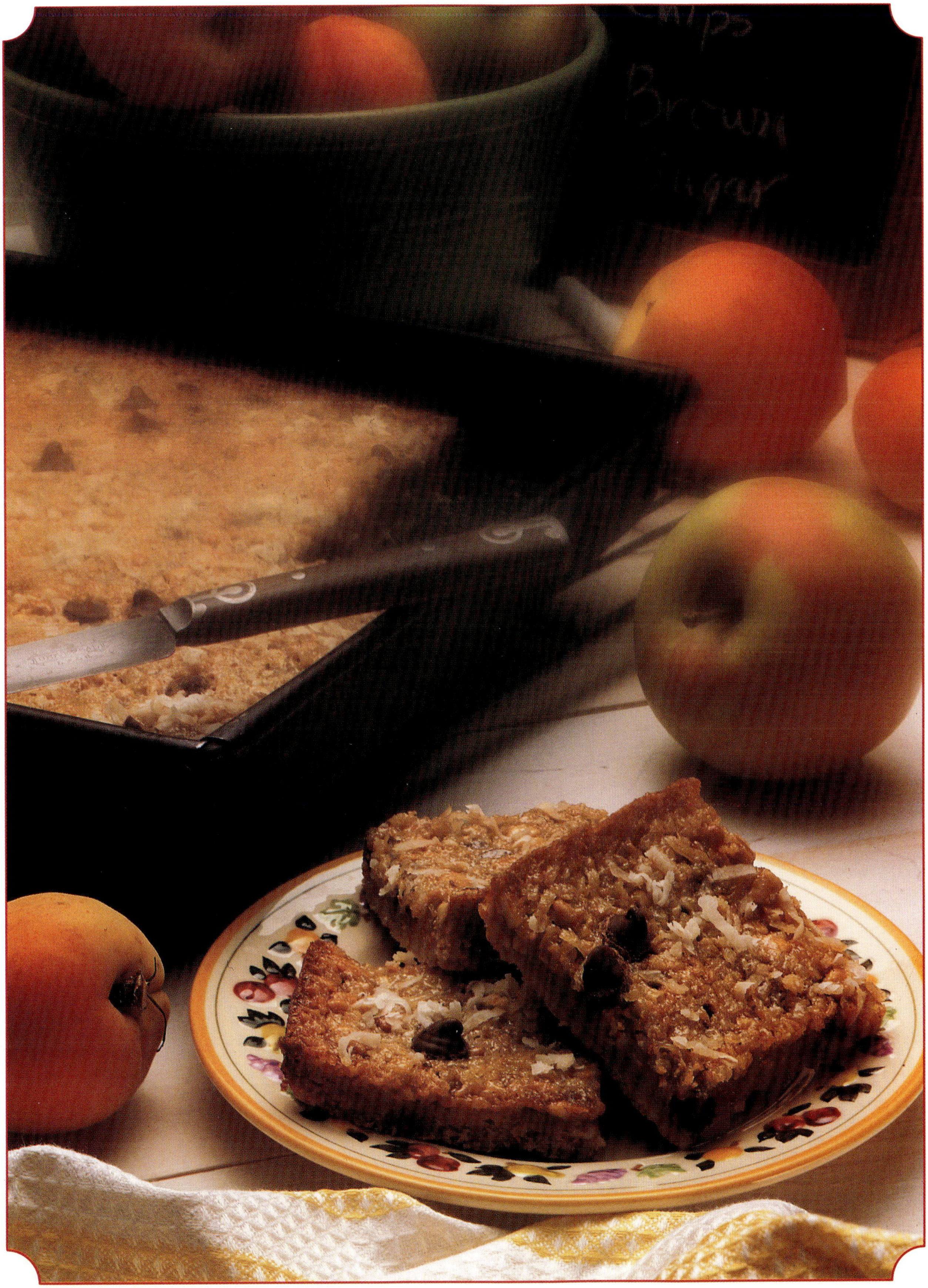
Brown

Peanut Butter Chocolate Chip Bars

Two all-time favorite flavors team up in these crunchy bars.

Preparation time: 45 minutes • Baking time: 12 minutes • Chilling time: 1 hour

Bars
- ¾ cup firmly packed brown sugar
- ½ cup sugar
- 1 cup LAND O LAKES® Butter, softened
- 1 egg
- 1½ teaspoons vanilla
- 2¼ cups all-purpose flour
- 1 teaspoon baking soda
- ½ teaspoon salt
- 1 cup chopped salted peanuts
- 1 cup semi-sweet real chocolate chips

Topping
- 1 cup semi-sweet real chocolate chips
- ½ cup creamy peanut butter
- ½ cup chopped salted peanuts

Heat oven to 375°. In large mixer bowl combine brown sugar, sugar, butter, egg and vanilla. Beat at medium speed, scraping bowl often, until well mixed (1 to 2 minutes). Reduce speed to low; add flour, baking soda and salt. Continue beating until well mixed (1 to 2 minutes). By hand, stir in 1 cup peanuts and 1 cup chocolate chips. Press on bottom of greased 15x10x1-inch jelly roll pan. Bake for 12 to 17 minutes or until edges are lightly browned.

Meanwhile, in 1-quart saucepan melt 1 cup chocolate chips and peanut butter. Cook over low heat, stirring constantly, until smooth (4 to 5 minutes). Spread over warm bars; sprinkle with ½ cup chopped peanuts. Cover; refrigerate until topping sets (about 1 hour). Cut into bars; store covered at room temperature. **YIELD:** 60 bars.

Nutrition Information (1 bar): Calories 130; Protein 2g; Carbohydrate 12g; Fat 8g; Cholesterol 10mg; Sodium 110mg

Peanut Butter Squares

This rich peanut filling sits atop a delicate butter crust for a mouth-watering bar resembling peanut pie.

Preparation time: 30 minutes • Baking time: 32 minutes

Crust
- 1 cup all-purpose flour
- 1/3 cup sugar
- 1/2 cup LAND O LAKES® Butter, softened
- 1/4 cup salted peanuts, chopped

Filling
- 1/2 cup sugar
- 1/4 cup creamy peanut butter
- 1/2 cup light corn syrup
- 2 eggs
- 1/4 teaspoon salt
- 1/2 teaspoon vanilla
- 1 cup salted peanuts

Heat oven to 350°. In small mixer bowl combine all crust ingredients except chopped peanuts. Beat at low speed, scraping bowl often, until crumbly (1 to 2 minutes). By hand, stir in 1/4 cup chopped peanuts. Press on bottom of 9-inch square baking pan. Bake for 12 to 17 minutes or until edges are lightly browned.

Meanwhile, in same mixer bowl combine all filling ingredients except peanuts. Beat at low speed, scraping bowl often, until well mixed (1 to 2 minutes). By hand, stir in 1 cup peanuts; pour filling over hot partially baked crust. Continue baking for 20 to 30 minutes or until filling is lightly browned and set. Cool completely; cut into bars. **YIELD:** 25 bars.

Nutrition Information (1 bar): Calories 170; Protein 4g; Carbohydrate 18g; Fat 9g; Cholesterol 30mg; Sodium 150mg

Brownies

～

The fudgy goodness of our Old-Fashioned Brownies never disappoints the loyal fan. But until you've tried our other deliciously decadent varieties, you can't truly consider yourself a connoisseur! Enjoy "educating" yourself with Irish Mist Brownies, Crazy-Topped Brownies and Fruit-Filled White Chocolate Brownies.

Fruit-Filled White Chocolate Brownies, see page 84

Fruit-Filled White Chocolate Brownies

Apricots, cranberries and raisins fill these white chocolate brownies.

Preparation time: 45 minutes • Baking time: 40 minutes
(pictured on page 83)

- ½ cup LAND O LAKES® Butter
- 1 (12-ounce) package (2 cups) vanilla milk chips*
- 2 eggs
- ¼ cup sugar
- 1¼ cups all-purpose flour
- ⅓ cup orange juice
- ½ teaspoon salt
- ⅓ cup chopped dried apricots
- ⅓ cup chopped cranberries
- ¼ cup golden raisins
- 2 tablespoons firmly packed brown sugar
- ⅓ cup chopped walnuts, toasted

Heat oven to 325°. In 1-quart saucepan melt butter. Remove from heat. Add 1 cup vanilla milk chips; do not stir. Set aside.

In large mixer bowl beat eggs at medium speed until foamy (1 to 2 minutes). Increase speed to high; add sugar. Beat, scraping bowl often, until thick and lemon colored (2 to 3 minutes). Reduce speed to low; add reserved butter and vanilla chip mixture, flour, orange juice and salt. Continue beating, scraping bowl often, until just combined (1 minute). Spread half of batter (about 1¼ cups) into greased and floured 9-inch square baking pan. Bake for 15 to 18 minutes or until edges are light golden brown.

Sprinkle apricots, cranberries, raisins and brown sugar over hot partially baked brownies. Stir remaining 1 cup vanilla milk chips into remaining batter; spread over fruit. (Some fruit may show through batter.) Sprinkle with walnuts. Bake for 25 to 35 minutes or until edges are light golden brown. Cool completely; cut into bars.
YIELD: 25 brownies.

* 12 ounces white chocolate, chopped, can be substituted for 1 (12-ounce) package (2 cups) vanilla milk chips.

Nutrition Information (1 brownie): Calories 170; Protein 3g; Carbohydrate 19g; Fat 10g; Cholesterol 25mg; Sodium 110mg

Chocolate Chunk Orange Blonde Brownies

These "blonde" brownies are butterscotch flavored with chunks of milk chocolate and a hint of orange.

Preparation time: 30 minutes • Baking time: 20 minutes

- ¾ cup LAND O LAKES® Butter, melted
- ⅔ cup sugar
- ½ cup firmly packed brown sugar
- 1 egg
- 1 teaspoon grated orange peel
- 2 cups all-purpose flour
- ½ teaspoon baking powder
- ½ teaspoon baking soda
- ½ teaspoon salt
- 6 ounces milk chocolate, broken into ½-inch pieces

Heat oven to 350°. In 2-quart saucepan melt butter over medium heat (2 to 4 minutes). Remove from heat. Stir in sugar, brown sugar, egg and orange peel until well mixed. Stir in all remaining ingredients <u>except</u> chocolate. Gently stir in chocolate pieces. Spread batter into greased 9-inch square baking pan. Bake for 20 to 25 minutes or until toothpick inserted in center comes out clean. Cool completely; cut into bars.
YIELD: 25 brownies.

Nutrition Information (1 brownie): Calories 160; Protein 2g; Carbohydrate 21g; Fat 8g; Cholesterol 25mg; Sodium 140mg

Crazy-Topped Brownies

An all-time favorite jazzed up with peanut butter frosting and toppings of your choice.

Preparation time: 35 minutes • Baking time: 20 minutes • Cooling time: 30 minutes

Brownies
- ½ cup LAND O LAKES® Butter
- 2 (1-ounce) squares unsweetened baking chocolate
- 1 cup sugar
- ¾ cup all-purpose flour
- 2 eggs

Frosting
- 1 cup powdered sugar
- ⅓ cup peanut butter
- 1½ teaspoons vanilla
- 2 to 3 tablespoons milk

Toppings
- Semi-sweet chocolate chips, raisins, salted peanuts, etc.

Heat oven to 350°. In 2-quart saucepan melt butter and unsweetened chocolate over medium heat, stirring constantly, until smooth (4 to 6 minutes). Stir in sugar, flour and eggs until well mixed. Spread into greased 9-inch square baking pan. Bake for 20 to 25 minutes or until brownie begins to pull away from sides of pan. DO NOT OVERBAKE. Cool completely.

In small mixer bowl combine all frosting ingredients except milk. Beat at medium speed, gradually adding enough milk for desired spreading consistency. Spread over cooled brownies.

Sprinkle with any combination of desired toppings (about 1 cup total); press lightly into frosting. Cut into bars. **YIELD:** 25 brownies.

Nutrition Information (1 brownie without topping): Calories 160; Protein 2g; Carbohydrate 20g; Fat 10g; Cholesterol 26mg; Sodium 60mg

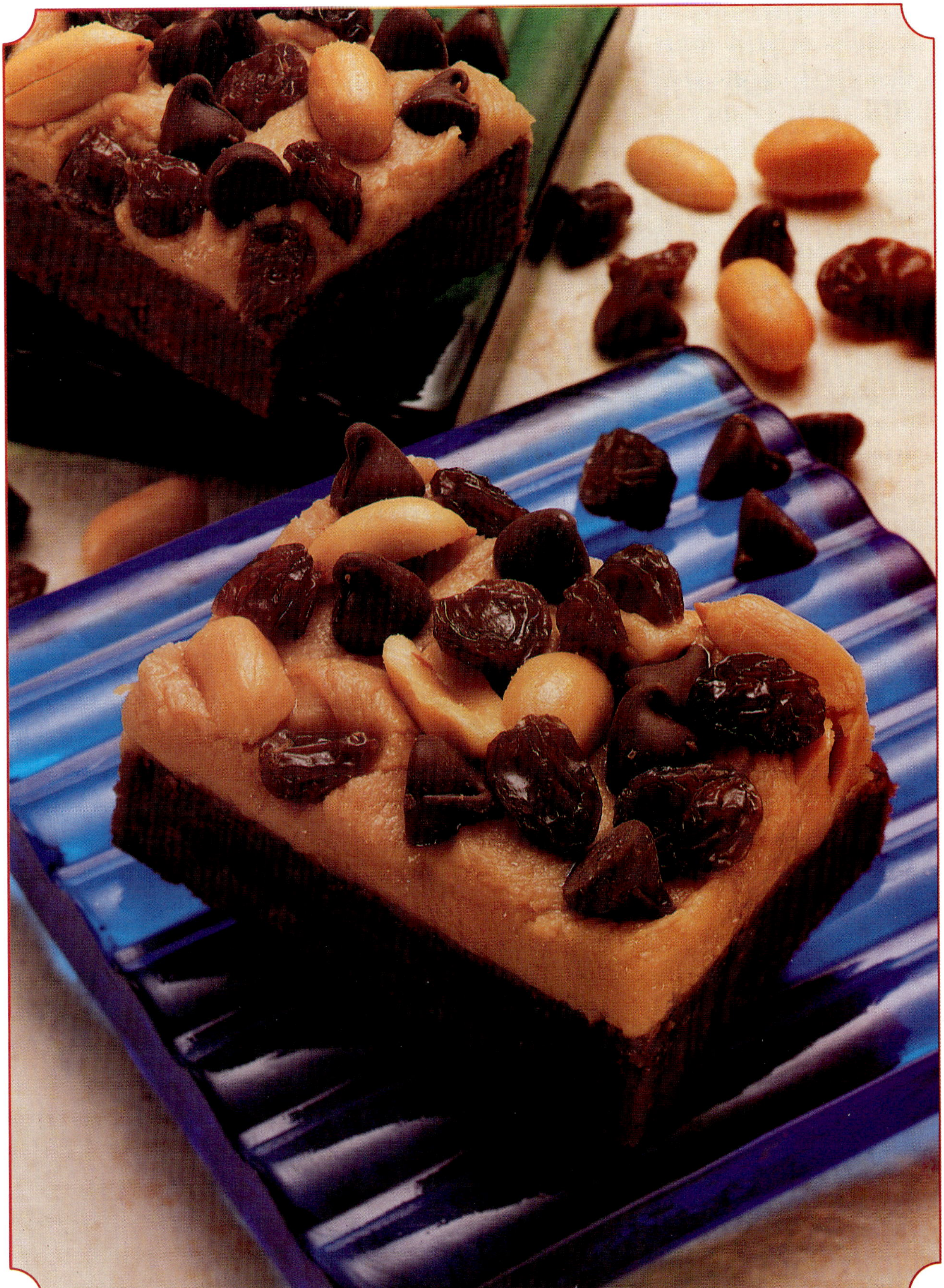

Double Fudge Cream Cheese Brownies

Two kinds of chocolate and cream cheese make these homemade brownies absolutely yummy.

Preparation time: 15 minutes • Baking time: 30 minutes

Brownies
- 1 cup LAND O LAKES® Butter
- 4 (1-ounce) squares unsweetened baking chocolate
- 2 cups sugar
- 1½ cups all-purpose flour
- 4 eggs, slightly beaten
- 1 teaspoon baking powder
- 1 teaspoon salt
- 2 teaspoons vanilla
- 1 cup semi-sweet chocolate chips

Filling
- ¼ cup sugar
- 2 tablespoons LAND O LAKES® Butter, softened
- 1 (3-ounce) package cream cheese, softened
- 1 egg
- 1 tablespoon all-purpose flour
- ½ teaspoon vanilla

Heat oven to 350°. In 2-quart saucepan melt 1 cup butter and unsweetened chocolate over medium heat, stirring occasionally, until smooth (4 to 6 minutes). Stir in all remaining brownie ingredients <u>except</u> chocolate chips. Fold in chocolate chips. Spread half of batter into greased 13x9-inch baking pan.

In small mixer bowl combine all filling ingredients. Beat at medium speed, scraping bowl often, until creamy. Spread over brownie mixture. Spoon remaining batter over cream cheese mixture. (Some cream cheese mixture may show through batter.) Bake for 30 to 35 minutes or until brownie begins to pull away from sides of pan. Cool completely; cut into bars. Store refrigerated. **YIELD:** 36 brownies.

Nutrition Information (1 brownie): Calories 180; Protein 2g; Carbohydrate 20g; Fat 11g; Cholesterol 50mg; Sodium 140mg

Old-Fashioned Brownies

Brownies, a favorite in every family, are quick, easy and delicious.

Preparation time: 20 minutes • Baking time: 20 minutes

- 2 cups all-purpose flour
- 2 cups sugar
- 1/2 cup unsweetened cocoa
- 1 cup LAND O LAKES® Butter, softened
- 2 eggs
- 1 teaspoon vanilla
- 1 cup chopped walnuts **or** pecans

Heat oven to 350°. In large mixer bowl combine all ingredients <u>except</u> walnuts. Beat at low speed, scraping bowl often, until well mixed (1 to 2 minutes). By hand, stir in walnuts. Spread into greased 13x9-inch baking pan. Bake for 20 to 25 minutes or until brownie begins to pull away from sides of pan. Cool completely; cut into bars.

YIELD: 36 brownies.

Nutrition Information (1 brownie): Calories 140; Protein 2g; Carbohydrate 17g; Fat 8g; Cholesterol 26mg; Sodium 60mg

Irish Mist Brownies

A fudgy brownie, layered with mint butter cream and drizzled with chocolate.

Preparation time: 30 minutes • Baking time: 25 minutes • Cooling time: 30 minutes

Brownies
- ½ cup LAND O LAKES® Butter
- 2 (1-ounce) squares unsweetened baking chocolate
- 1 cup sugar
- ¾ cup all-purpose flour
- 2 eggs

Filling
- 2 cups powdered sugar
- 3 tablespoons LAND O LAKES® Butter, softened
- 1 (3-ounce) package cream cheese, softened
- ½ teaspoon peppermint extract
- 5 drops green food coloring
- 2 drops yellow food coloring

- 1 (1-ounce) square unsweetened baking chocolate, melted

Heat oven to 350°. In 2-quart saucepan melt ½ cup butter and 2 squares chocolate over medium heat, stirring constantly, until smooth (4 to 6 minutes). Stir in all remaining brownie ingredients until well mixed. Spread into greased 9-inch square baking pan. Bake for 25 to 30 minutes or until brownie begins to pull away from sides of pan. Cool completely.

In small mixer bowl combine all filling ingredients <u>except</u> chocolate. Beat at medium speed, scraping bowl often, until creamy (2 to 3 minutes). Spread over cooled bars. Drizzle with melted chocolate. Cool completely; cut into bars. Store refrigerated.
YIELD: 25 brownies.

Nutrition Information (1 brownie): Calories 160; Protein 2g; Carbohydrate 20g; Fat 9g; Cholesterol 35mg; Sodium 65mg

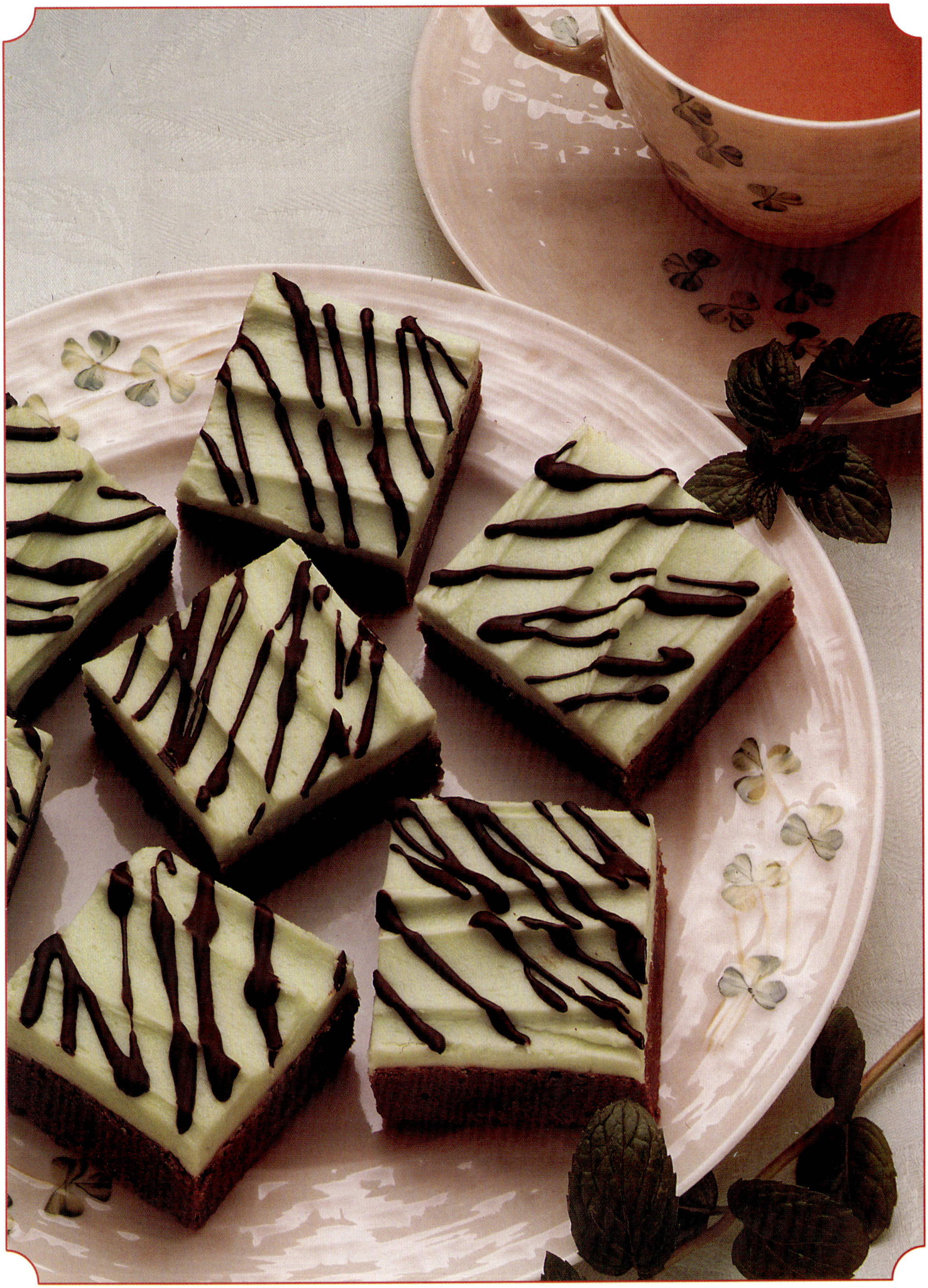

Triple Chocolate Fudge Brownies

Milk Chocolate, semi-sweet chocolate and white chocolate combine in this chocolate lover's delight.

Preparation time: 15 minutes • Baking time: 20 minutes • Cooling time: 30 minutes

Brownies
- 2/3 cup semi-sweet real chocolate chips
- 1/4 cup LAND O LAKES® Butter
- 1/2 teaspoon instant coffee granules
- 2 tablespoons warm water
- 1/2 cup sugar
- 3 eggs
- 1/2 cup all-purpose flour
- 3 tablespoons unsweetened cocoa
- 1 teaspoon vanilla
- 1/2 cup coarsely chopped macadamia nuts

Glaze
- 1/2 cup semi-sweet real chocolate chips
- 2 tablespoons LAND O LAKES® Butter
- 2 tablespoons light corn syrup
- 1 tablespoon milk
- 1/2 cup powdered sugar

Drizzle
- 2 tablespoons milk chocolate chips, melted
- 2 tablespoons vanilla milk chips, melted*
- 2 teaspoons vegetable oil

Heat oven to 350°. In 1-quart saucepan melt 2/3 cup chocolate chips and 1/4 cup butter over low heat, stirring occasionally (3 to 4 minutes); set aside.

In small bowl stir together coffee granules and water until coffee is dissolved; set aside.

In small mixer bowl combine sugar and eggs. Beat at high speed, scraping bowl often, until thick and lemon colored (1 to 2 minutes). By hand, stir in melted chocolate chip mixture, dissolved coffee and all remaining brownie ingredients. Pour batter into greased and floured 9-inch square baking pan. Bake for 20 to 25 minutes or until toothpick inserted in center comes out clean. Cool completely.

Meanwhile, in 1-quart saucepan melt 1/2 cup chocolate chips and 2 tablespoons butter over low heat, stirring occasionally, until smooth (3 to 4 minutes). Remove from heat. With wire whisk, stir in corn syrup and milk until smooth. Stir in powdered sugar until smooth. Spread glaze over cooled brownies.

In small bowl stir together melted milk chocolate chips and 1 teaspoon oil. In small bowl stir together melted vanilla milk chips and 1 teaspoon oil. Drizzle both mixtures over brownies; pull knife through glaze to create design. Cut into bars. **YIELD:** 25 brownies.

* 1/2 ounce white chocolate, melted, can be substituted for 2 tablespoons vanilla milk chips, melted.

Nutrition Information (1 brownie): Calories 140; Protein 2g; Carbohydrate 15g; Fat 9g; Cholesterol 35mg; Sodium 45mg

Rocky Road Fudge Brownies

A rich fudge brownie topped with butterscotch, marshmallows and peanuts.

Preparation time: 20 minutes • Baking time: 32 minutes

Brownies
- ½ cup LAND O LAKES® Butter
- 2 (1-ounce) squares unsweetened baking chocolate
- 2 eggs
- 1 cup sugar
- ⅔ cup all-purpose flour
- ¼ teaspoon salt
- 1 teaspoon vanilla

Topping
- ½ cup chopped salted peanuts
- ½ cup butterscotch-flavored chips
- 1 cup miniature marshmallows
- ¼ cup chocolate-flavored topping

Heat oven to 350°. In 1-quart saucepan melt butter and chocolate over low heat, stirring occasionally, until smooth (8 to 10 minutes); set aside.

In small mixer bowl beat eggs at medium speed until thick and lemon colored (2 to 3 minutes). Continue beating, gradually adding cooled chocolate mixture and remaining brownie ingredients and scraping bowl often, until well mixed (1 to 2 minutes). Spread into greased 9-inch square baking pan. Bake for 20 to 25 minutes or until brownie begins to pull away from sides of pan.

Sprinkle peanuts, butterscotch chips and marshmallows over hot brownies. Drizzle with chocolate topping. Continue baking for 12 to 18 minutes or until lightly browned. Cool completely; cut into bars.
YIELD: 25 brownies.

Nutrition Information (1 brownie): Calories 150; Protein 2g; Carbohydrate 18g; Fat 8g; Cholesterol 30mg; Sodium 100mg

Nutty Caramel Layer Brownies

Pecans, chocolate and caramels create an all-time favorite brownie.

Preparation time: 30 minutes • Baking time: 35 minutes • Cooling time: 15 minutes

Caramel
- 1/3 cup evaporated milk
- 1 (14-ounce) package caramels, unwrapped

Brownies
- 1/2 cup firmly packed brown sugar
- 1/2 cup sugar
- 1 cup LAND O LAKES® Butter, softened
- 3 eggs
- 1 (4-ounce) bar sweet cooking chocolate, melted
- 1 teaspoon vanilla
- 1 1/2 cups all-purpose flour
- 1/2 cup chopped pecans

- 1 (11 1/2-ounce) package (2 cups) milk chocolate chips
- 1 cup coarsely chopped pecans

Heat oven to 350°. In 2-quart saucepan combine evaporated milk and caramels. Cook over medium heat, stirring occasionally, until caramels are melted (6 to 8 minutes); set aside.

In large mixer bowl combine brown sugar, sugar and butter. Beat at medium speed, scraping bowl often, until creamy (2 to 3 minutes). Add eggs, chocolate and vanilla. Continue beating, scraping bowl often, until well mixed (1 to 2 minutes). Reduce speed to low; add flour. Continue beating, scraping bowl often, until just combined (1 minute). By hand, stir in 1/2 cup chopped pecans. Spread 2 1/2 cups batter into greased 13x9-inch baking pan. Bake 15 minutes.

Sprinkle chocolate chips over hot partially baked brownie; spread caramel mixture over chips. Spoon remaining batter over caramel mixture; spread. (Batter may not cover all of caramel mixture.) Sprinkle 1 cup pecans over batter. Bake for 20 to 30 minutes or until toothpick inserted at angle in top layer of brownie comes out clean. Cool 15 minutes; refrigerate until set. Cut into bars.
YIELD: 36 brownies.

Nutrition Information (1 brownie): Calories 240; Protein 3g; Carbohydrate 27g; Fat 14g; Cholesterol 35mg; Sodium 95mg

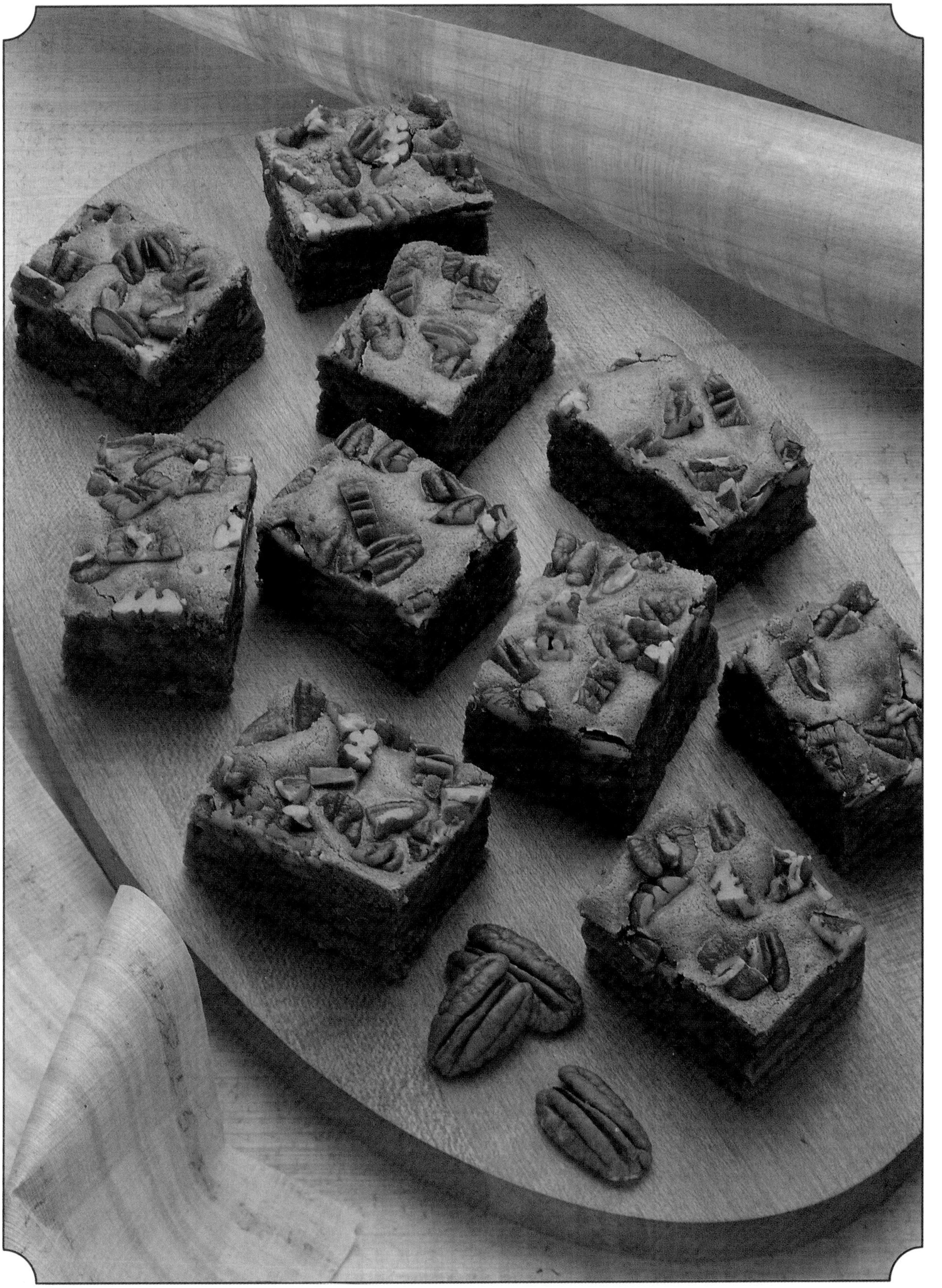

Toffee Candy Bar Brownies

Chopped candy bars add extra flavor to this traditional brownie.

Preparation time: 15 minutes • Baking time: 25 minutes

¼	cup LAND O LAKES® Butter
1	cup sugar
6	tablespoons unsweetened cocoa
2	eggs
¾	cup all-purpose flour
5	ounces (5 to 6 bars) chopped chocolate coated toffee candy bars

Heat oven to 350°. In 2-quart saucepan melt butter over medium heat (1 to 2 minutes). Remove from heat. Stir in all remaining ingredients until well mixed. Pour into greased and floured 9-inch square baking pan. Bake for 20 to 25 minutes or until firm to the touch. Cool completely; cut into bars. **YIELD:** 25 brownies.

Nutrition Information (1 brownie): Calories 100; Protein 1g; Carbohydrate 15g; Fat 5g; Cholesterol 22mg; Sodium 50mg

Chocolate Chip Peanut Butter Brownies

A rich brownie with kids' favorite flavors—peanut butter and chocolate.

Preparation time: 15 minutes • Baking time: 30 minutes

- 1 cup sugar
- ½ cup LAND O LAKES® Butter, melted
- ⅓ cup chunky peanut butter
- 2 eggs
- 1 teaspoon vanilla
- 1¼ cups all-purpose flour
- ⅔ cup semi-sweet chocolate chips

Heat oven to 350°. In medium bowl stir together sugar, butter, peanut butter, eggs and vanilla until well mixed. Stir in flour until well mixed. Stir in chocolate chips. Spread into greased 9-inch square baking pan. Bake for 25 to 30 minutes or until lightly browned. Cool completely.
YIELD: 16 brownies.

Nutrition Information (1 brownie): Calories 210; Protein 3g; Carbohydrate 25g; Fat 12g; Cholesterol 40mg; Sodium 95mg

Holiday & Specialty Cookies & Bars

You'll probably find these recipes too tempting to save for just once a year. In that case, turn any day into a special occasion! Invent a holiday of your own, or simply invite the neighbors over to share Cinnamon Coffee Cookies, Melt-In-Your-Mouth Spritz or Snow-Topped Peppermint Bars.

White & Dark Chocolate Layered Cookies, see page 100; Melt-In-Your-Mouth Spritz, see page 101; Black Walnut Ice Box Cookies, see page 102

White & Dark Chocolate Layered Cookies

White and dark chocolate dough are layered, then sliced for a delicious and attractive cookie.

Preparation time: 30 minutes • Chilling time: 4 hours • Baking time: 8 minutes
(pictured on page 97)

2½ cups all-purpose flour
1¼ cups sugar
1 cup LAND O LAKES® Butter, softened
1 egg
¼ teaspoon salt
2 teaspoons vanilla
1 (3-ounce) bar white chocolate, melted
3 (1-ounce) squares semi-sweet baking chocolate, melted

In large mixer bowl combine all ingredients except white chocolate and semi-sweet chocolate. Beat at low speed, scraping bowl often, until well mixed (1 to 2 minutes). Remove half of dough; set aside. Add melted white chocolate to dough in bowl; beat at low speed until well mixed (1 to 2 minutes). Remove dough from bowl; place on 12-inch piece of waxed paper. Place reserved half of dough in mixer bowl; add melted semi-sweet chocolate. Beat at low speed until well mixed (1 to 2 minutes). Place dough on 12-inch piece of waxed paper. Shape each piece of dough into 5-inch square; wrap in plastic food wrap. Freeze 1 hour or refrigerate until firm (at least 2 hours).

Cut each 5-inch square into quarters (forming 2½-inch squares). On lightly floured pieces of 15-inch waxed paper roll out each quarter to equal 10x4-inch rectangle. Place all 8 pieces of waxed paper with dough on top of each other on a cookie sheet; cover with plastic food wrap. Freeze 15 minutes or refrigerate until firm (at least 1 hour).

Place one piece of waxed paper with dough on counter. Brush dough surface lightly with water. Flip alternating color of rolled out dough on top of wet dough; remove waxed paper. Press lightly to seal dough together. Continue stacking dough, alternating colors and brushing dough lightly with water, until all 8 pieces of dough are stacked as evenly as possible. Cover with plastic food wrap; freeze 15 minutes or refrigerate until firm (at least 1 hour).

Heat oven to 375°. Unwrap dough. With sharp knife, trim off ends of dough stack to make even. With sharp knife, cut ¼-inch slices of dough; trim uneven ends (reserve all scraps of trimmed dough). Cut each cookie strip in half. Using spatula, place on cookie sheets. Bake for 8 to 10 minutes or until edges are very lightly browned. DO NOT OVERBAKE. Let stand 1 minute; remove from cookie sheets. Press together reserved scraps to make marbleized dough. On lightly floured surface roll out dough to ¼-inch thickness. Cut with 2-inch cookie cutters. Bake as directed above.
YIELD: 6 dozen cookies.

Nutrition Information (1 cookie): Calories 70; Protein 1g; Carbohydrate 8g; Fat 3g; Cholesterol 10mg; Sodium 35mg

Melt-In-Your-Mouth Spritz

Perfect spritz cookies every time, plus five variations to create variety.

Preparation time: 1 hour • Baking time: 6 minutes
(pictured on page 97)

- 2/3 cup sugar
- 1 cup LAND O LAKES® Butter, softened
- 1 egg
- 1/2 teaspoon salt
- 2 teaspoons vanilla
- 2 1/4 cups all-purpose flour

Heat oven to 400°. In large mixer bowl combine all ingredients <u>except</u> flour. Beat at medium speed, scraping bowl often, until mixture is creamy (2 to 3 minutes). Reduce speed to low; add flour. Continue beating, scraping bowl often, until well mixed (2 to 3 minutes). If desired, add ingredients from one of the following variations. If dough is too soft, cover; refrigerate until firm enough to form cookies (30 to 45 minutes). Place dough in cookie press; form desired shapes 1 inch apart on cookie sheets. Bake for 6 to 8 minutes or until edges are lightly browned. **YIELD:** 5 dozen cookies.

VARIATIONS

<u>Spiced Spritz</u>: To dough add 1 teaspoon cinnamon, 1 teaspoon nutmeg, 1/2 teaspoon allspice and 1/4 teaspoon cloves. Glaze: In small bowl stir together 1 cup powdered sugar, 2 tablespoons milk and 1/2 teaspoon vanilla until smooth; drizzle over warm cookies.

<u>Eggnog Spritz</u>: To dough add 1 teaspoon nutmeg. Glaze: In small bowl stir together 1 cup powdered sugar, 1/4 cup softened LAND O LAKES® Butter, 2 tablespoons water and 1/4 teaspoon rum extract until smooth; drizzle over warm cookies.

<u>Piña Colada Spritz</u>: Omit vanilla in dough recipe above. Add 1 tablespoon pineapple juice and 1/4 teaspoon rum extract; stir in 1/2 cup finely chopped flaked coconut. Frosting: In small mixer bowl combine 1 cup powdered sugar, 2 tablespoons softened LAND O LAKES® Butter, 2 tablespoons pineapple preserves and 1 tablespoon pineapple juice. Beat at medium speed, scraping bowl often, until creamy (2 to 3 minutes). Spread on cooled cookies. If desired, sprinkle with toasted coconut.

<u>Chocolate Mint Spritz</u>: To dough add 1/4 teaspoon mint extract. Immediately after removing cookies from oven place 1 chocolate candy kiss on each cookie.

<u>Chocolate Flecked Spritz</u>: To dough add 1/4 cup coarsely grated semi-sweet chocolate.

Nutrition Information (1 cookie): Calories 50; Protein 1g; Carbohydrate 6g; Fat 3g; Cholesterol 10m; Sodium 50mg

Black Walnut Ice Box Cookies

Black walnuts have a somewhat strong, slightly bitter flavor which completes these brown sugar cookies.

Preparation time: 45 minutes • Chilling time: 2 hours • Baking time: 6 minutes
(pictured on page 97)

- 3½ cups all-purpose flour
- 2 cups firmly packed brown sugar
- 1 cup LAND O LAKES® Butter, softened
- 2 eggs
- 1½ teaspoons baking soda
- ½ teaspoon salt
- ½ teaspoon vanilla
- ½ cup chopped black walnuts or walnuts

In large mixer bowl combine all ingredients <u>except</u> walnuts. Beat at low speed, scraping bowl often, until well mixed (3 to 4 minutes). By hand, stir in walnuts. Divide dough in half; on lightly floured surface shape each half into 10-inch roll (about 1½-inch diameter). Wrap in plastic food wrap; refrigerate until firm (at least 2 hours).

<u>Heat oven to 400°</u>. Cut rolls into ⅛-inch slices. Place 1 inch apart on cookie sheets. Bake for 6 to 8 minutes or until lightly browned.
YIELD: 8 dozen cookies.

Nutrition Information (1 cookie): Calories 60; Protein 1g; Carbohydrate 8g; Fat 2g; Cholesterol 10mg; Sodium 50mg

Applesauce Raisin Bars

This moist and buttery applesauce bar is topped with a fluffy butter pecan frosting.

Preparation time: 30 minutes • Baking time: 25 minutes • Cooling time: 1 hour
(pictured on page 105)

Bars
- 1 cup sugar
- 1/3 cup LAND O LAKES® Butter, softened
- 1 egg
- 1 1/2 cups all-purpose flour
- 1 1/2 cups applesauce
- 1 teaspoon allspice
- 1 teaspoon cinnamon
- 3/4 teaspoon baking soda
- 1/2 teaspoon salt
- 1/2 cup raisins

Frosting
- 1/4 cup LAND O LAKES® Butter, softened
- 2 cups powdered sugar
- 1/8 teaspoon allspice
- 1/8 teaspoon cinnamon
- 2 tablespoons milk
- 2 teaspoons vanilla
- 1/2 cup chopped pecans

Heat oven to 350°. In large mixer bowl combine sugar, 1/3 cup butter and egg. Beat at medium speed, scraping bowl often, until creamy (1 to 2 minutes). Reduce speed to low; add flour, applesauce, allspice, cinnamon, baking soda and salt. Continue beating, scraping bowl often, until well mixed (2 to 3 minutes). By hand, stir in raisins. Spoon batter into greased 13x9-inch baking pan. Bake for 25 to 35 minutes or until toothpick inserted in center comes out clean. Cool completely.

In small mixer bowl combine all frosting ingredients <u>except</u> pecans. Beat at medium speed, scraping bowl often, until smooth (1 to 2 minutes). By hand, gently stir in pecans. Frost cooled bars; cut into bars. **YIELD:** 48 bars.

Nutrition Information (1 bar): Calories 80; Protein 1g; Carbohydrate 14g; Fat 3g; Cholesterol 10mg; Sodium 65mg

Chocolate Drizzled Cherry Bars

The favorite combination of chocolate and cherry makes these bars delicious.

Preparation time: 30 minutes • Baking time: 42 minutes

Crumb Mixture
- 2 cups all-purpose flour
- 2 cups quick-cooking oats
- 1½ cups sugar
- 1¼ cups LAND O LAKES® Butter, softened

Filling
- 1 (21-ounce) can cherry fruit filling
- 1 teaspoon almond extract

Glaze
- ½ cup semi-sweet real chocolate chips
- 1 tablespoon shortening

Heat oven to 350°. In large mixer bowl combine all crumb mixture ingredients. Beat at low speed, scraping bowl often, until mixture is crumbly (1 to 2 minutes). Reserve 1½ cups crumb mixture; press remaining crumb mixture on bottom of 13x9-inch baking pan. Bake for 15 to 20 minutes or until edges are very lightly browned.

Meanwhile, in same bowl stir together fruit filling and almond extract. Spread filling over hot partially baked crust; sprinkle with reserved crumb mixture. Continue baking for 27 to 32 minutes or until lightly browned.

In 1-quart saucepan melt chocolate chips and shortening over low heat, stirring occasionally, until smooth (2 to 3 minutes). Drizzle glaze over bars. Cool completely; cut into bars.
YIELD: 36 bars.

TIP: Bars can be cut into shapes other than squares and rectangles. Try cutting into diamonds or triangles for gift giving.

Nutrition Information (1 bar): Calories 160; Protein 2g; Carbohydrate 22g; Fat 8g; Cholesterol 15mg; Sodium 70mg

Chocolate Drizzled Cherry Bars; Applesauce Raisin Bars, see page 103

Cinnamon N' Sugar Shortbread

This flaky shortbread is made extra special with a sprinkling of cinnamon and sugar.

Preparation time: 30 minutes • Baking time: 20 minutes

Shortbread

1¾	cups all-purpose flour
¾	cup powdered sugar
½	cup cake flour
1	cup LAND O LAKES® Butter, softened
½	teaspoon cinnamon

Topping

1	tablespoon sugar
⅛	teaspoon cinnamon

Heat oven to 350°. In large bowl combine all shortbread ingredients. With fork, stir together until soft dough forms. Press evenly on bottom of 2 (9-inch) pie pans.

In small bowl stir together topping ingredients; sprinkle over shortbread. Score each into 8 wedges; prick all over with fork. Bake for 20 to 30 minutes or until light golden brown. Cool on wire cooling rack; cut into wedges. **YIELD:** 16 cookies.

TIP: 2 (9-inch) shortbread molds can be used in place of 2 (9-inch) pie pans. Do not sprinkle with topping before baking. After removing from mold, sprinkle with topping.

Nutrition Information (1 cookie): Calories 190; Protein 2g; Carbohydrate 19g; Fat 12g; Cholesterol 30mg; Sodium 120mg

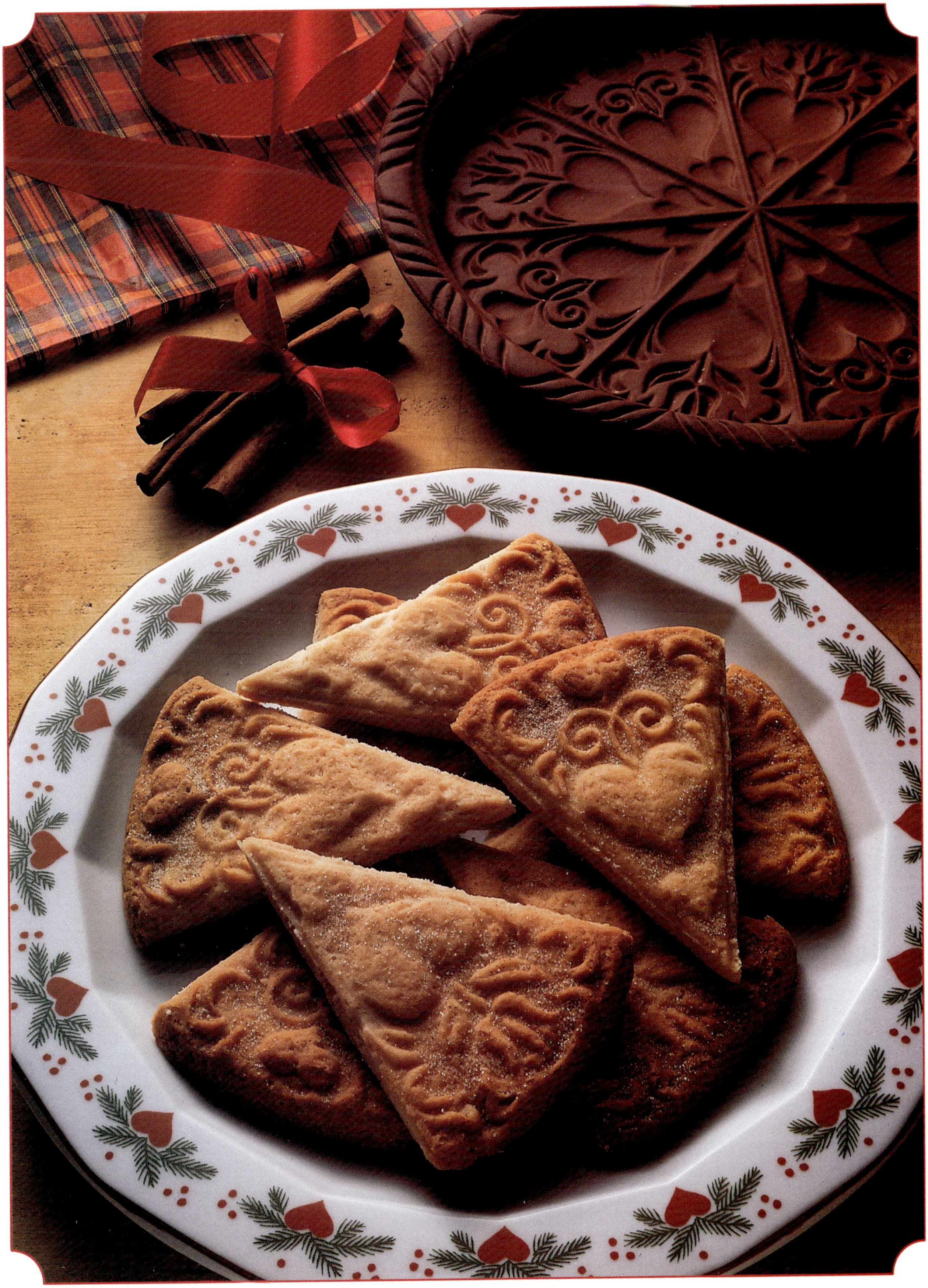

Cranberry Hazelnut Biscotti

Toasted hazelnuts and dried cranberries combine to make delicious, crisp biscotti cookies.

Preparation time: 30 minutes • Baking time: 39 minutes • Cooling time: 15 minutes

2	cups all-purpose flour
1/2	cup (2 1/2 ounces) hazelnuts *or* filberts, toasted, skins removed, finely chopped
1/2	teaspoon baking powder
1/2	teaspoon baking soda
1/4	teaspoon salt
3/4	cup sugar
2	eggs
1/4	cup vegetable oil
2	teaspoons grated orange peel
1	tablespoon orange juice
1 1/2	teaspoons vanilla
2/3	cup (3 ounces) finely chopped dried cranberries
1 to 2	teaspoons all-purpose flour
1	egg white
1	tablespoon water
	Sugar

Heat oven to 350°. In medium bowl combine 2 cups flour, hazelnuts, baking powder, baking soda and salt; set aside. In large mixer bowl combine 3/4 cup sugar and eggs. Beat at medium speed, scraping bowl often, until thick and lemon colored (2 to 3 minutes). Add vegetable oil, orange peel, orange juice and vanilla. Continue beating until well mixed (1 to 2 minutes). Reduce speed to low. Continue beating, gradually adding flour mixture, until well mixed (1 to 2 minutes). By hand, stir in dried cranberries.

Turn dough onto lightly floured surface (dough will be soft and sticky). Sprinkle lightly with 1 to 2 teaspoons flour; knead flour into dough. With floured hands shape into 2 (8x2-inch) logs. Place 3 to 4 inches apart on greased cookie sheet; flatten tops slightly. Combine egg white and water; brush over top of biscotti. Sprinkle with sugar. Bake for 23 to 30 minutes or until lightly browned and firm to the touch. Let cool on cookie sheet 15 minutes.

<u>Reduce oven temperature to 300°</u>. With serrated knife, cut logs diagonally into 1/2-inch slices; arrange slices, cut-side down, on cookie sheets. Bake for 8 to 10 minutes; turn slices. Continue baking for 8 to 10 minutes or until golden brown. Remove to wire cooling rack; cool completely. **YIELD:** 2 1/2 dozen cookies.

Nutrition Information (1 cookie): Calories 70; Protein 1g; Carbohydrate 10g; Fat 3g; Cholesterol 10mg; Sodium 40mg

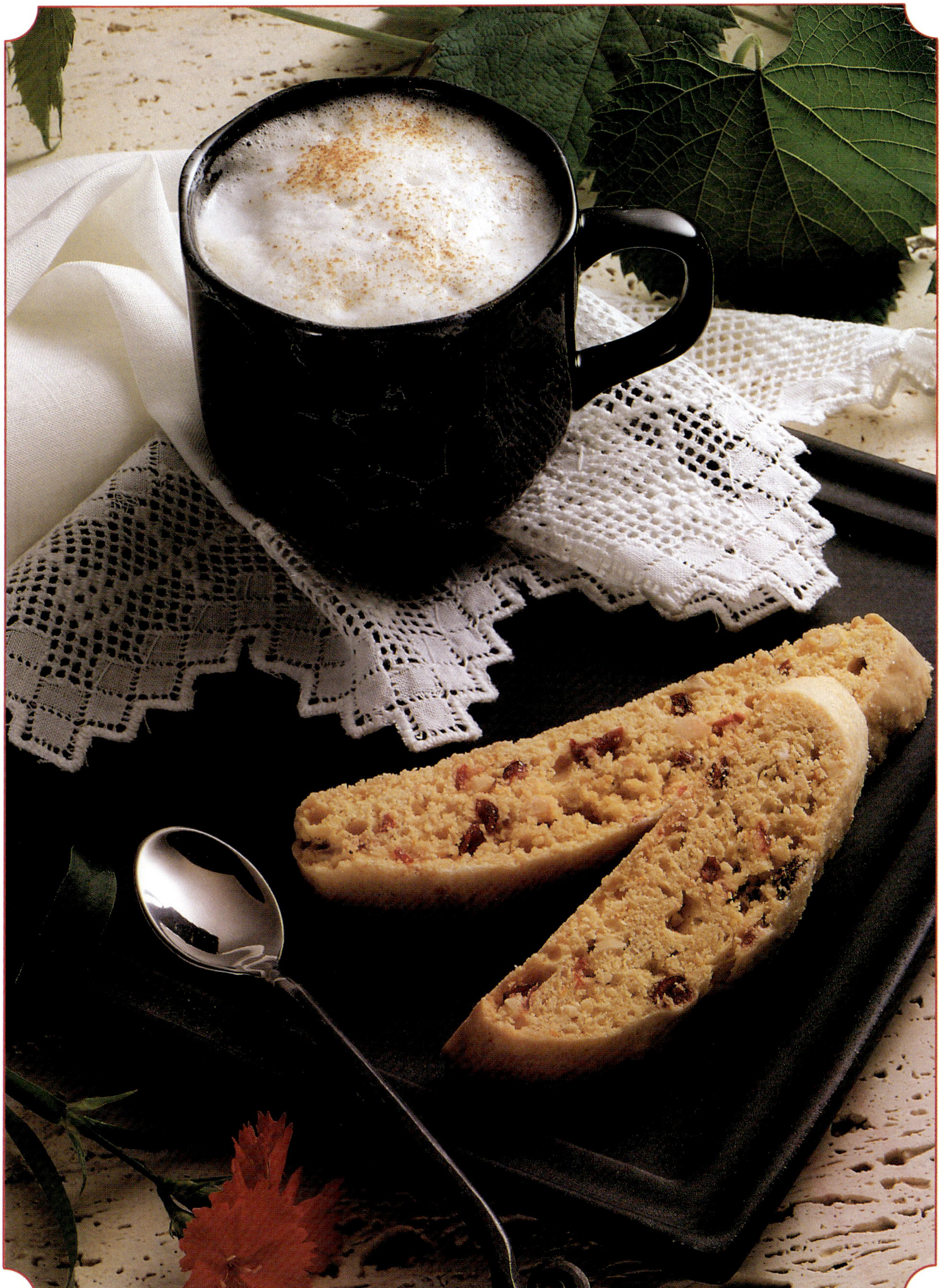

Creamy Lemon Medallions

Tender lemon cookies are filled with a buttery lemon filling.

Preparation time: 1 hour • Chilling time: 1 hour • Baking time: 7 minutes • Cooling time: 15 minutes

Cookies

- 1 cup sugar
- 1 cup LAND O LAKES® Butter, softened
- 1 egg, separated, <u>reserve white</u>
- 2 teaspoons grated lemon peel
- 2 tablespoons lemon juice
- 1 teaspoon vanilla
- 2¼ cups all-purpose flour
- ¼ teaspoon salt

- 1 reserved egg white
- 1 tablespoon water
- Sugar

Filling

- 2¼ cups powdered sugar
- 3 tablespoons LAND O LAKES® Butter, softened
- 1 tablespoon grated lemon peel
- 1 tablespoon lemon juice
- 1 teaspoon vanilla
- 2 to 4 teaspoons milk

In large mixer bowl combine 1 cup sugar and 1 cup butter. Beat at medium speed, scraping bowl often, until creamy (1 to 2 minutes). Add egg yolk, lemon peel, lemon juice and vanilla. Beat at medium speed, scraping bowl often, 1 minute. Reduce speed to low; add flour and salt. Continue beating, scraping bowl often, until well mixed (1 to 2 minutes). Divide dough in half; wrap in plastic food wrap. Refrigerate until firm (at least 1 hour).

<u>Heat oven to 350°</u>. On lightly floured surface roll out dough, half at a time (keeping remaining dough refrigerated), to ⅛-inch thickness. Cut with 1½-inch cookie cutter. Place ½ inch apart on greased cookie sheets. With fork prick surface of each cookie several times. Meanwhile, in small bowl stir together egg white and water. Lightly brush surface of cookies with egg white mixture. Sprinkle lightly with sugar. Bake for 7 to 10 minutes or until lightly browned. Cool completely.

In small mixer bowl combine all filling ingredients <u>except</u> milk. Beat at low speed, gradually adding enough milk for desired spreading consistency. Put cookies together in pairs with about <u>1 teaspoonful</u> filling for each medallion. **YIELD:** 4 dozen cookies.

Nutrition Information (1 cookie): Calories 100; Protein 1g; Carbohydrate 14g; Fat 5g; Cholesterol 15mg; Sodium 60mg

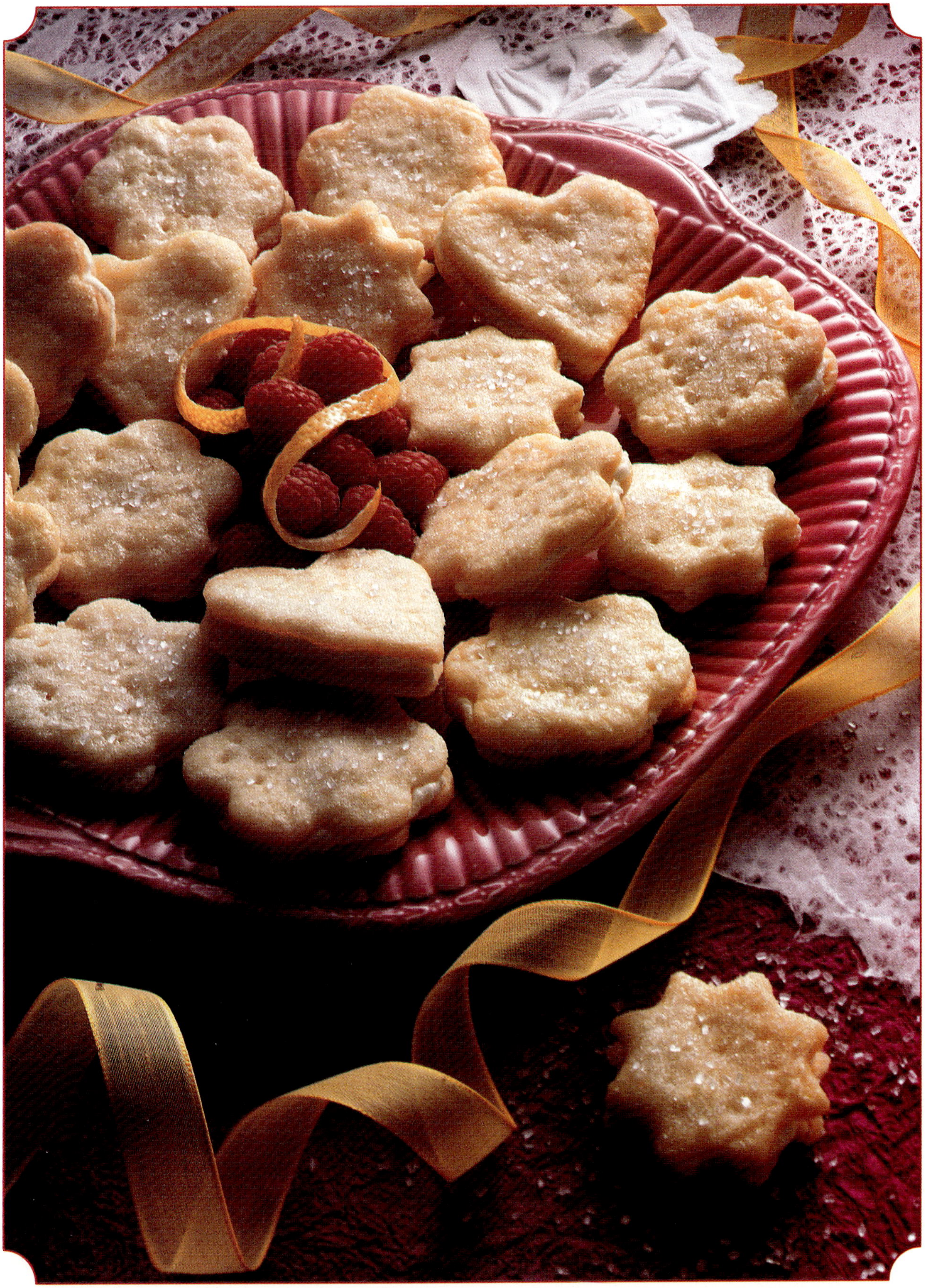

Holiday Chocolate Butter Cookies

A rich, chocolate butter cookie with endless possibilities.

Preparation time: 1 hour • Baking time: 7 minutes

Cookies
- 1/2 cup sugar
- 3/4 cup LAND O LAKES® Butter, softened
- 1 egg yolk
- 1 teaspoon almond extract
- 1 1/2 cups all-purpose flour
- 1/4 cup unsweetened cocoa

Suggested Coatings
- Semi-sweet real chocolate chips, melted
- Vanilla-flavored candy coating, melted

Suggested Toppings
- Finely chopped almonds, pecans or walnuts
- Candy coated milk chocolate pieces
- Flaked coconut
- Fruit preserves
- Colored sugars
- Multicolored decorator candies
- Maraschino cherries

Heat oven to 375°. In large mixer bowl combine all cookie ingredients except flour and cocoa. Beat at medium speed, scraping bowl often, until mixture is creamy (2 to 3 minutes). Reduce speed to low. Continue beating, gradually adding flour and cocoa, until well mixed (2 to 3 minutes). Shape dough according to choice of variation directions. Bake for 7 to 9 minutes or until set. **YIELD:** 3 dozen cookies.

VARIATIONS

Nut Rolls: Shape dough into 2 to 3-inch logs. Place 1 inch apart on cookie sheets. Bake as directed above. Cool completely. Dip both ends of each cookie in melted chocolate chips, then in finely chopped nuts.

Fruit Filled: Shape dough into 1-inch balls. Place 1 inch apart on cookie sheets. Make a depression in center of each cookie with back of teaspoon. Bake as directed above. Cool completely. Fill centers with fruit preserves.

Decorated: Shape rounded teaspoonfuls of dough into desired forms (logs, balls, flattened, etc.). Place 1 inch apart on cookie sheets. Bake as directed above. Cool completely. Drizzle cookies with melted chocolate chips or melted vanilla coating. Decorate with finely chopped nuts, coconut, colored sugars or multicolored decorator candies.

Surprise Filled: Shape dough into 1-inch balls. Place 1 inch apart on cookie sheets. Make a depression in center of each cookie with back of teaspoon. Bake as directed above. Cool completely. Place one of the following ingredients in center of each cookie: nut, candy coated milk chocolate piece, maraschino cherry half or 1/2 teaspoon flaked coconut. Spoon melted chocolate chips over filled center. Let stand to harden chocolate.

Snowballs: Shape dough into 1-inch balls. Place 1 inch apart on cookie sheets. Bake as directed above. Roll in powdered sugar or unsweetened cocoa while still warm and again when cool.

Nutrition Information (1 cookie): Calories 130; Protein 2g; Carbohydrate 10g; Fat 10g; Cholesterol 15mg; Sodium 45mg

Snow-Topped Peppermint Bars

A sprinkling of powdered sugar creates the "snow" on top of these refreshing bars.

Preparation time: 45 minutes • Baking time: 20 minutes

- 2 cups all-purpose flour
- 2/3 cup sugar
- 1 cup LAND O LAKES® Butter, softened
- 1/2 cup milk
- 1 egg
- 1 teaspoon baking powder
- 1 teaspoon vanilla
- 1/3 cup crushed starlight peppermint candy

Powdered sugar

Heat oven to 375°. In large mixer bowl combine all ingredients except crushed peppermint candy and powdered sugar. Beat at low speed, scraping bowl often, until well mixed (2 to 3 minutes). By hand, stir in crushed peppermint candy. Pour into greased and floured 13x9-inch baking pan. Bake for 20 to 25 minutes or until toothpick inserted in center comes out clean. Cool completely; sprinkle with powdered sugar. Cut into bars. **YIELD:** 36 bars.

Nutrition Information (1 bar): Calories 90; Protein 1g; Carbohydrate 11g; Fat 5g; Cholesterol 20mg; Sodium 65mg

Czechoslovakian Kolache Cookies

A yeast-flavored dough is rolled, cut and filled with fruit preserves for an attractive holiday cookie.

Preparation time: 1 hour • Baking time: 10 minutes • Cooling time: 30 minutes

Cookies

1/2	cup milk
1	cup LAND O LAKES® Butter, cold
3	cups all-purpose flour
1/4	cup sugar
1/2	teaspoon salt
1	(1/4-ounce) package active dry yeast
1	egg
1	teaspoon vanilla
1/2	cup cherry preserves*
1	egg, well beaten

Glaze

2/3	cup powdered sugar
1	teaspoon almond extract
2 to 3	teaspoons milk

Heat oven to 350°. In 1-quart saucepan heat milk until just comes to a boil; let cool to warm (105 to 115°F).

Meanwhile, in large mixer bowl cut butter into chunks; add flour, sugar and salt. Beat at low speed, scraping bowl often, until mixture resembles coarse crumbs (30 to 60 seconds). Dissolve yeast in warm milk. Stir in egg and vanilla. Add milk mixture to flour mixture. Beat at low speed, scraping bowl often, until well mixed (1 to 2 minutes). Divide dough in half.

On lightly floured surface roll out dough, half at a time, to 1/8 to 1/4-inch thickness. Cut dough into 3-inch squares. Place <u>1 teaspoon</u> cherry preserves on each square. Bring up 2 opposite corners of each square to center; pinch tightly to hold together. Place on greased cookie sheets; brush with beaten egg. Bake for 10 to 14 minutes or until golden brown. Remove to wire cooling rack; cool completely. In small bowl combine powdered sugar and almond extract. Gradually stir in enough milk for desired spreading consistency. Drizzle over cookies. **YIELD:** 2 dozen cookies.

* 1/2 cup of your favorite flavor preserves can be substituted for 1/2 cup cherry preserves.

Nutrition Information (1 cookie): Calories 170; Protein 3g; Carbohydrate 22g; Fat 8g; Cholesterol 40mg; Sodium 130mg

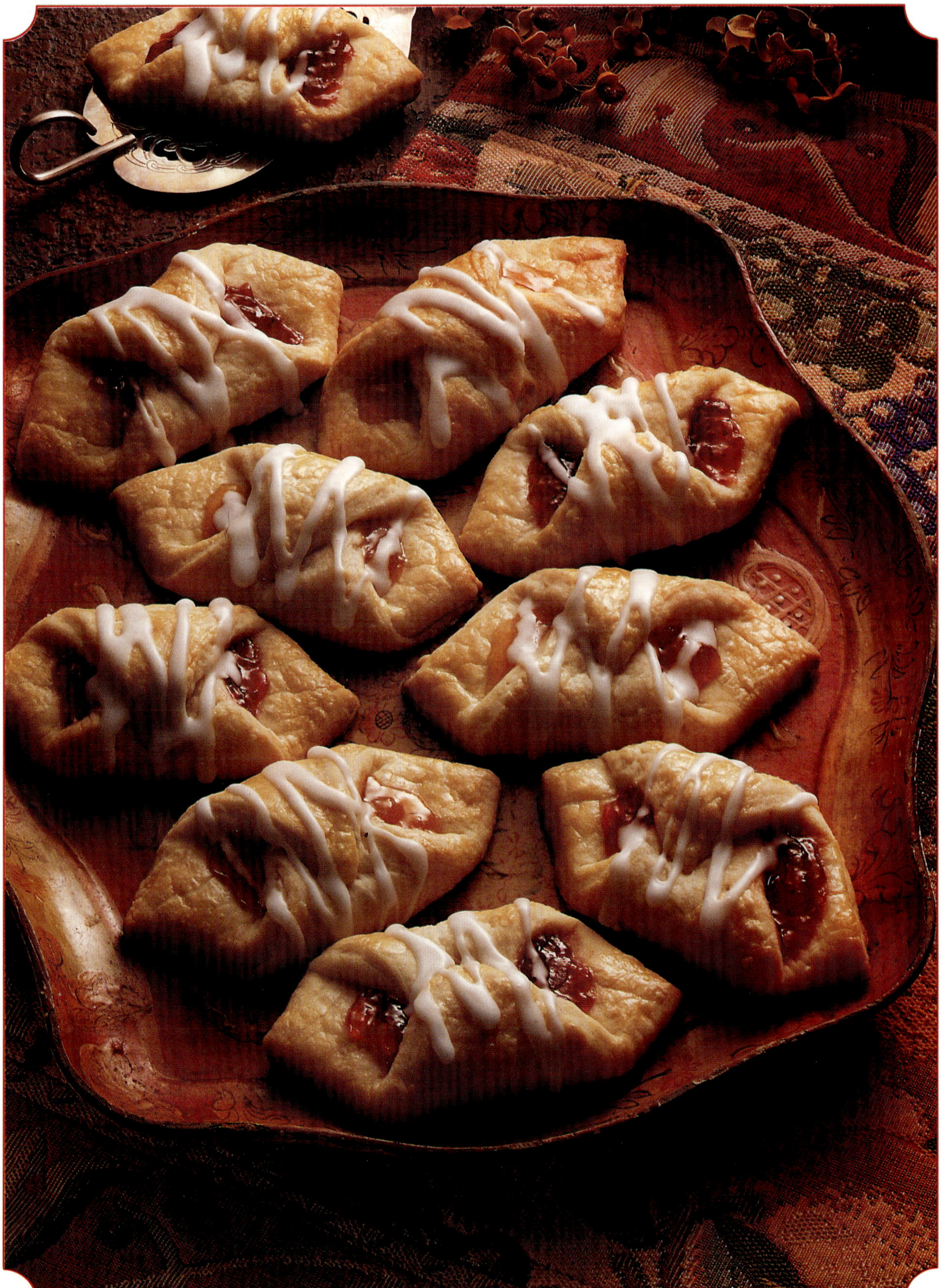

Favorite Butter Cookies

These crisp, tender cutout cookies can be decorated to capture the spirit of your occasion.

Preparation time: 1 hour 30 minutes • Chilling time: 2 hours • Baking time: 6 minutes • Cooling time: 15 minutes

Cookies
- 2½ cups all-purpose flour
- 1 cup sugar
- 1 cup LAND O LAKES® Butter, softened
- 1 egg
- 1 teaspoon baking powder
- 2 tablespoons orange juice
- 1 tablespoon vanilla

Frosting
- 4 cups powdered sugar
- ½ cup LAND O LAKES® Butter, softened
- 2 teaspoons vanilla
- 3 to 4 tablespoons milk

Decorations
- Food coloring
- Colored sugars
- Flaked coconut
- Cinnamon candies

In large mixer bowl combine all cookie ingredients. Beat at low speed, scraping bowl often, until well mixed (1 to 2 minutes). If desired, divide dough into thirds; color two-thirds of dough with desired food colorings. Cover; refrigerate until firm (at least 2 hours).

Heat oven to 400°. On lightly floured surface roll out dough, one-third at a time (keeping remaining dough refrigerated), to ¼-inch thickness. Cut with 3-inch cookie cutters. Place 1 inch apart on cookie sheets. If desired, sprinkle colored sugars on some of the cookies or bake and decorate later. Bake for 6 to 10 minutes or until edges are lightly browned. Cool completely.

In small mixer bowl combine all frosting ingredients <u>except</u> milk. Beat at low speed, gradually adding enough milk for desired spreading consistency. Frost or decorate cooled cookies. **YIELD:** 3 dozen cookies.

TIP: To use cookies as ornaments, while cookies are still warm use toothpick to make hole in top of each cookie. Cool and decorate. Thread ribbon or thread through holes in cookies.

Nutrition Information (1 cookie): Calories 170; Protein 1g; Carbohydrate 23g; Fat 8g Cholesterol 25mg; Sodium 90mg

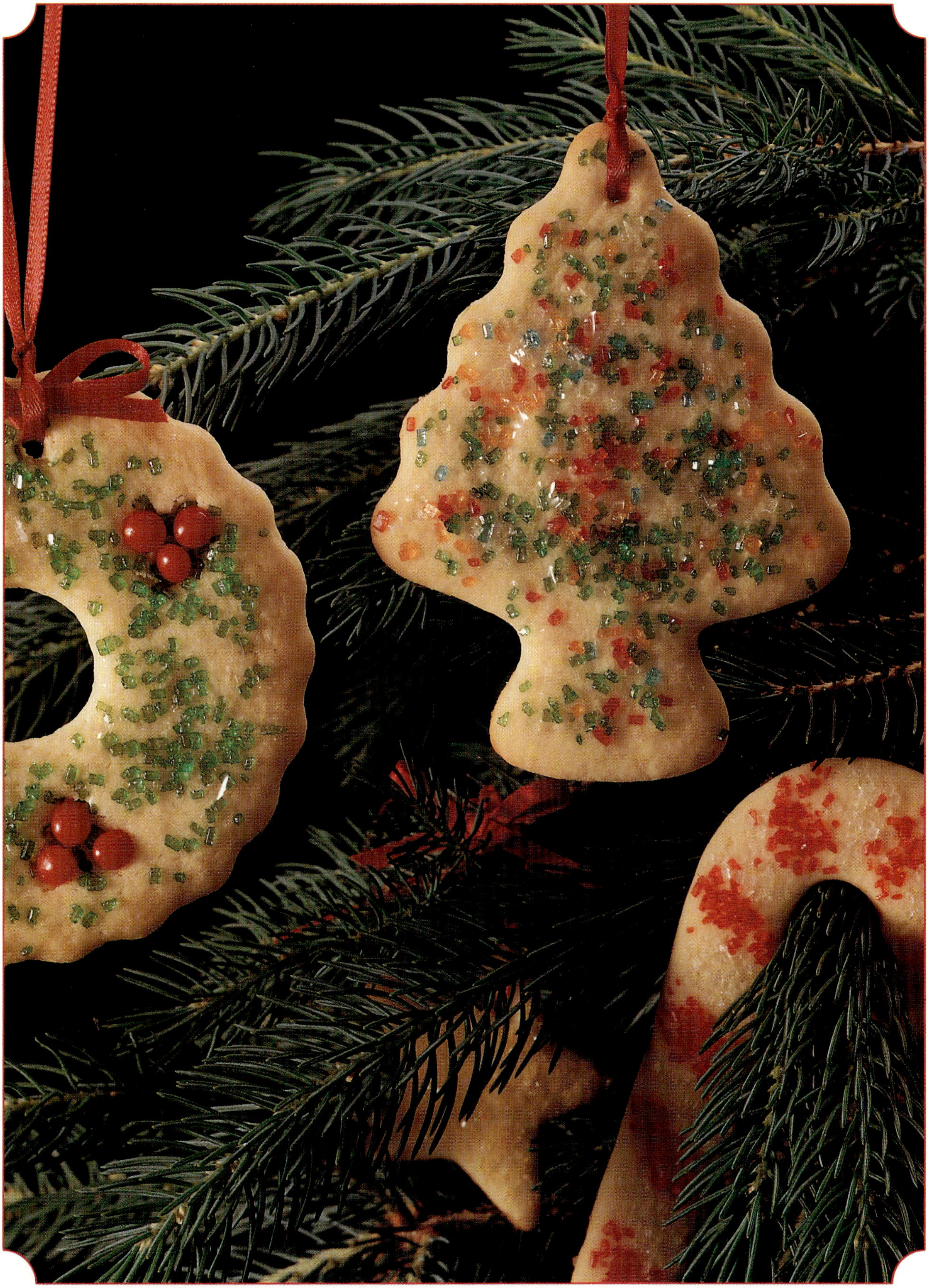

Frosted Pumpkin Bars

Cream cheese frosting complements these moist pumpkin bars.

Preparation time: 1 hour 15 minutes • Baking time: 30 minutes • Cooling time: 30 minutes

Bars
- 1½ cups sugar
- ¾ cup LAND O LAKES® Butter, softened
- 1 (16-ounce) can (1¾ cups) pumpkin
- 4 eggs
- 2¼ cups all-purpose flour
- 2 teaspoons baking powder
- 1 teaspoon baking soda
- ½ teaspoon salt
- ½ teaspoon cinnamon
- 1 cup raisins

Frosting
- 3 cups powdered sugar
- ⅓ cup LAND O LAKES® Butter, softened
- 1 (3-ounce) package cream cheese, softened
- 2 to 3 tablespoons milk

Heat oven to 350°. In large mixer bowl combine sugar, butter, pumpkin and eggs. Beat at medium speed, scraping bowl often, until well mixed (1 to 2 minutes). Reduce speed to low; add flour, baking powder, soda, salt and cinnamon. Continue beating, scraping bowl often, until well mixed (1 to 2 minutes). By hand, stir in raisins. Pour into 15x10x1-inch jelly roll pan. Bake for 30 to 40 minutes or until toothpick inserted in center comes out clean. Cool completely.

In small mixer bowl combine all frosting ingredients <u>except</u> milk. Beat at medium speed, gradually adding enough milk for desired spreading consistency. Frost cooled bars; cut into bars. **YIELD:** 60 bars.

Nutrition Information (1 bar): Calories 110; Protein 1g; Carbohydrate 16g; Fat 4g; Cholesterol 25mg; Sodium 90mg

Cinnamon Coffee Cookies

Coffee powder, pecans and cinnamon flavor these easy slice-and-bake cookies.

Preparation time: 30 minutes • Chilling time: 1 hour • Baking time: 6 minutes

Cookies
- 1 cup firmly packed brown sugar
- 3/4 cup LAND O LAKES® Butter, softened
- 1/4 cup orange juice
- 1 tablespoon grated orange peel
- 2 3/4 cups all-purpose flour
- 1 tablespoon instant espresso coffee powder
- 1 3/4 teaspoons baking powder
- 1 teaspoon cinnamon
- 1/2 teaspoon salt
- 1/2 cup finely chopped pecans

Glaze
- 1 1/2 cups powdered sugar
- 3/4 teaspoon instant espresso coffee powder
- 3 to 4 tablespoons orange juice

- 96 chocolate covered coffee beans <u>or</u> chocolate dipped pecans, if desired

In large mixer bowl combine brown sugar and butter. Beat at medium speed, scraping bowl often, until creamy (1 to 2 minutes). Add 1/4 cup orange juice and orange peel. Beat at medium speed, scraping bowl often, until well mixed (1 to 2 minutes). Reduce speed to low; add all remaining cookie ingredients. Continue beating, scraping bowl often, until well mixed (1 to 2 minutes). Divide dough in half; shape each half into 15-inch roll (about 1 1/4-inch diameter). Wrap in plastic food wrap; refrigerate until firm (at least 1 hour).

<u>Heat oven to 375°</u>. Cut rolls into 1/4-inch slices. Place 1 inch apart on lightly greased cookie sheets. Flatten slightly with bottom of glass. Bake for 6 to 8 minutes or until edges are lightly browned.

Meanwhile, in small bowl combine powdered sugar and 3/4 teaspoon espresso powder. Gradually stir in enough orange juice for desired glazing consistency. Spoon about <u>1/4 teaspoon</u> glaze over each warm cookie; lightly press chocolate coated coffee bean on top of each cookie. **YIELD:** 8 dozen cookies.

Nutrition Information (1 cookie): Calories 45; Protein 1g; Carbohydrate 7g; Fat 2g; Cholesterol 5mg; Sodium 30mg

Holiday Thumbprint Cookies

Make a beautiful cookie tray using one cookie dough with many variations.

Preparation time: 1 hour • Baking time: 14 minutes

Cookies
- 2 cups all-purpose flour
- 1/2 cup firmly packed brown sugar
- 1 cup LAND O LAKES® Butter, softened
- 2 eggs, separated
- 1/8 teaspoon salt
- 1 teaspoon vanilla <u>or</u> almond extract

Suggested Coatings
- 1 1/2 cups finely chopped peanuts, almonds, pecans <u>or</u> walnuts
- Colored sugars
- Cinnamon and sugar

Suggested Toppings
- Chocolate stars
- Candied cherries
- Caramels, cut in half
- Maraschino cherries
- Fruit preserves

Heat oven to 350°. In large mixer bowl combine all cookie ingredients <u>except</u> egg whites. Beat at low speed, scraping bowl often, until well mixed (2 to 3 minutes). Shape rounded teaspoonfuls of dough into 1-inch balls.

In small bowl beat egg whites with fork until foamy. Dip each ball of dough into egg white; roll in choice of nuts. (If using colored sugars or cinnamon and sugar, do not dip balls of dough in egg white. Roll balls of dough in colored sugars or cinnamon and sugar.) Place 1 inch apart on greased cookie sheets. Make a depression in center of each cookie with back of teaspoon. Bake for 8 minutes.

Remove cookies from oven; fill centers with choice of suggested toppings. Continue baking for 6 to 10 minutes or until lightly browned. **YIELD:** 3 dozen cookies.

Nutrition Information (1 cookie): Calories 150; Protein 3g; Carbohydrate 12g; Fat 10g; Cholesterol 25mg; Sodium 70mg

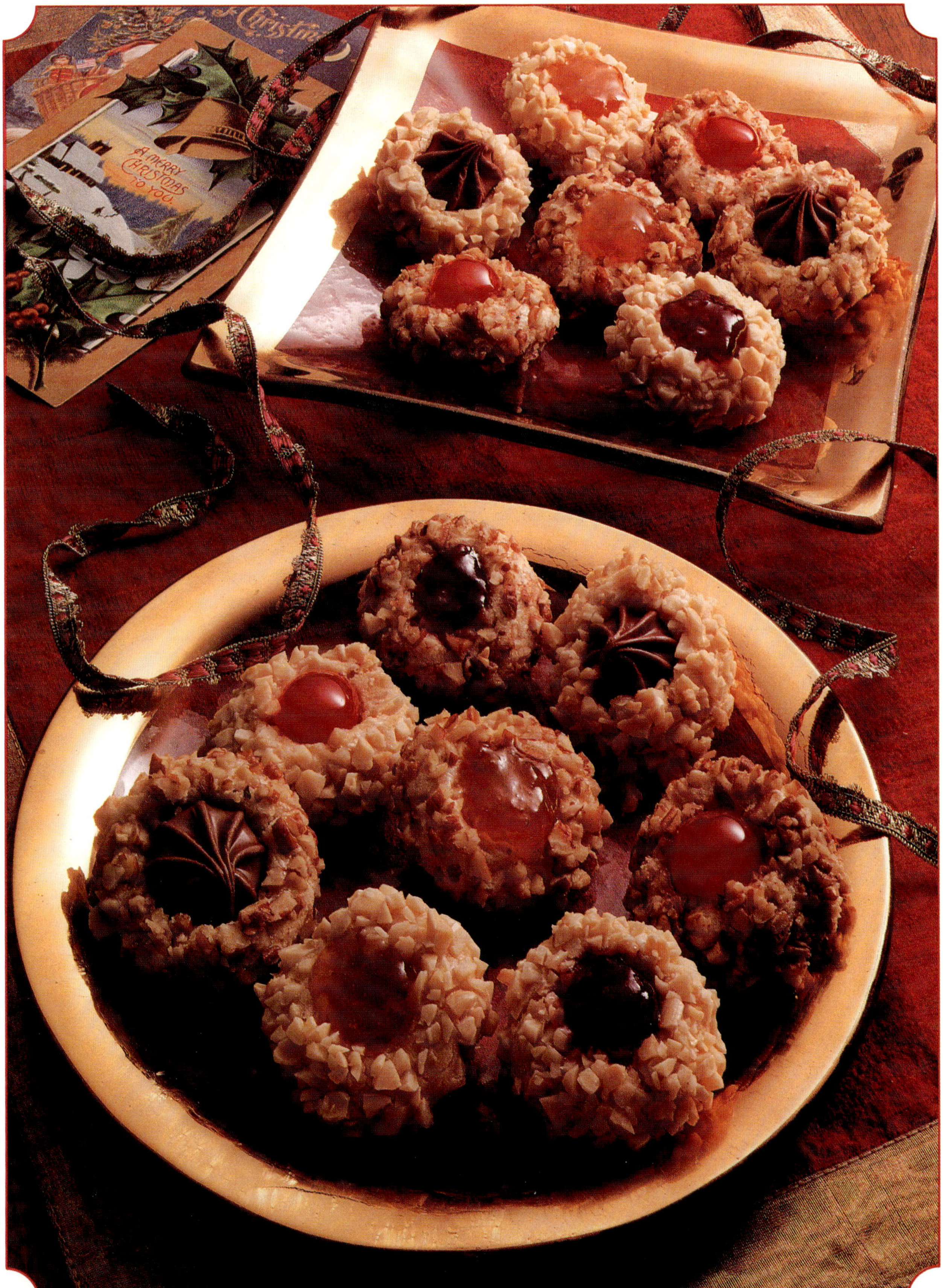
A MERRY CHRISTMAS TO YOU.

Snowball Cookies

A favorite at Christmastime, pecan-filled Snowball Cookies are scrumptious all year 'round.

Preparation time: 1 hour • Baking time: 18 minutes

- 2 cups all-purpose flour
- 2 cups finely chopped pecans
- 1/4 cup sugar
- 1 cup LAND O LAKES® Butter, softened
- 1 teaspoon vanilla

  Powdered sugar

Heat oven to 325°. In large mixer bowl combine all ingredients <u>except</u> powdered sugar. Beat at low speed, scraping bowl often, until well mixed (3 to 4 minutes). Shape rounded teaspoonfuls of dough into 1-inch balls. Place 1 inch apart on cookie sheets. Bake for 18 to 25 minutes or until very lightly browned. Cool 5 minutes. Roll in or sprinkle with powdered sugar while still warm and again when cool. **YIELD:** 3 dozen cookies.

Nutrition Information (1 cookie): Calories 130; Protein 1g; Carbohydrate 11g; Fat 9g; Cholesterol 15mg; Sodium 50mg

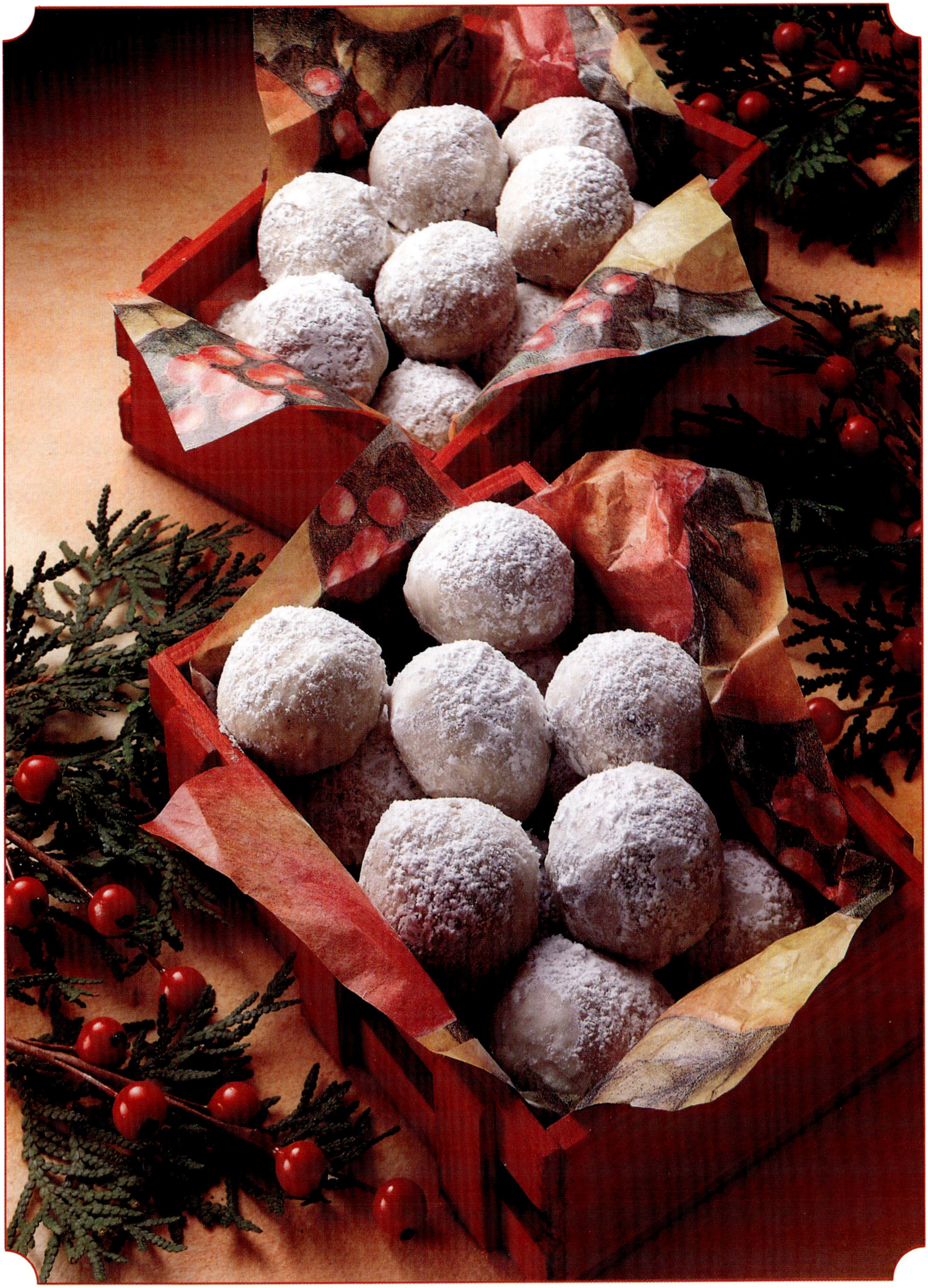

Mexican Chocolate Wedding Cakes

These cookies are a chocolate version of traditional Mexican wedding cakes.

Preparation time: 1 hour • Baking time: 8 minutes

- ¾ cup firmly packed brown sugar
- ¾ cup LAND O LAKES® Butter, softened
- 3 (1-ounce) squares unsweetened baking chocolate, melted
- 1 teaspoon vanilla
- 2 cups all-purpose flour
- 1 cup chopped nuts
- ½ teaspoon salt

Powdered sugar

Heat oven to 350°. In large mixer bowl combine brown sugar and butter. Beat at medium speed, scraping bowl often, until creamy (1 to 2 minutes). Add melted chocolate and vanilla. Continue beating, scraping bowl often, until well mixed (1 to 2 minutes). Reduce speed to low; add all remaining ingredients <u>except</u> powdered sugar. Continue beating, scraping bowl often, until well mixed (1 to 2 minutes). Shape rounded teaspoonfuls of dough into 1-inch balls. Place 2 inches apart on cookie sheets. Bake for 8 to 10 minutes or until set. Let stand 5 minutes; carefully remove from cookie sheets. Cool another 5 minutes. Roll in or sprinkle with powdered sugar while still warm and again when cool. **YIELD:** 5 dozen cookies.

Nutrition Information (1 cookie): Calories 70; Protein 1g; Carbohydrate 8g; Fat 4g; Cholesterol 5mg; Sodium 40mg

Teatime Sandwich Cookies

These delicate wafer cookies are paired together with a buttercream filling, forming a dainty treat for teatime.

Preparation time: 1 hour 30 minutes • Chilling time: 2 hours • Baking time: 6 minutes • Cooling time: 15 minutes

Cookies
- 2 cups all-purpose flour
- 1 cup LAND O LAKES® Butter, softened
- $1/3$ cup whipping cream

   Sugar

Filling
- $3/4$ cup powdered sugar
- $1/4$ cup LAND O LAKES® Butter, softened
- 1 teaspoon vanilla or almond extract
- 1 to 3 teaspoons milk

   Food coloring, if desired

In small mixer bowl combine all cookie ingredients except sugar. Beat at low speed, scraping bowl often, until well mixed (2 to 3 minutes). Divide dough into thirds; wrap in plastic food wrap. Refrigerate until firm (at least 2 hours).

Heat oven to 375°. On well floured surface roll out dough, one-third at a time (keeping remaining dough refrigerated), to $1/8$-inch thickness. Cut with $1 1/2$-inch round cookie cutter. Dip both sides of each cookie in sugar. Place 1 inch apart on cookie sheets; prick all over with fork. Bake for 6 to 9 minutes or until slightly puffy but not brown. Cool slightly; carefully remove from cookie sheets. Cool completely.

In small mixer bowl combine all filling ingredients except milk and food coloring. Beat at medium speed, gradually adding enough milk for desired spreading consistency. If desired, color filling with food coloring. Carefully put cookies together in pairs with scant $1/2$ teaspoonful filling for each sandwich. **YIELD:** $4 1/2$ dozen cookies.

Nutrition Information (1 cookie): Calories 70; Protein 1g; Carbohydrate 7g; Fat 5g; Cholesterol 15mg; Sodium 45mg

Index

A

ALMOND
Butter Rum Almond Crunch 9
Cheery Cherry Macaroons.....................27
Cherry Almond Chocolate Bars.............61
Graham Cracker Caramel Crisps...........69
Holiday Chocolate Butter Cookies.......112
Mocha Almond Bars 77
Strawberry Marzipan Bars.....................72

APPLESAUCE
Applesauce Raisin Bars 103

B

BANANA
Banana Cream Sandwich Cookies 28

BAR COOKIES, see also No-Bake Bar Cookies
Applesauce Raisin Bars 103
Caramel Chew Coconut Bars.................60
Caramel N' Chocolate Pecan Bars..........58
Caramel Rocky Road Bars......................62
Cheesecake Squares 56
Cherry Almond Chocolate Bars.............61
Chocolate Caramel Oatmeal Bars 64
Chocolate Drizzled Cherry Bars 104
Chocolate Meringue Peanut Bars...........65
English Toffee Bars 76
Frosted Orange Date Bars 57
Frosted Pumpkin Bars 118
Graham Cracker Caramel Crisps...........69
Grasshopper Butter Cream Bars............66
Lemon Coconut Bars 73
Lemon-Butter Bars 70
Mocha Almond Bars 77
Old-World Raspberry Bars.....................68
Peanut Brittle Bars..................................74
Peanut Butter Chocolate Bars 78
Peanut Butter Chocolate Chip Bars........80
Peanut Butter Squares 81
Snow-Topped Peppermint Bars 113
Strawberry Marzipan Bars.....................72

BISCOTTI
Cranberry Hazelnut Biscotti 108

BROWNIES
Chocolate Chip Peanut Butter Brownies....................................97
Chocolate Chunk Orange Blonde Brownies...............................85
Crazy-Topped Brownies.........................86
Double Fudge Cream Cheese Brownies................................88
Fruit-Filled White Chocolate Brownies..........................84
Irish Mist Brownies 90
Nutty Caramel Layer Brownies..............94
Old-Fashioned Brownies 89
Rocky Road Fudge Brownies 93
Toffee Candy Bar Brownies 96
Triple Chocolate Fudge Brownies..........92

C

CARAMEL
Caramel Chew Coconut Bars.................60
Caramel N' Chocolate Pecan Bars..........58
Caramel Rocky Road Bars......................62
Chocolate Caramel & Nut Treats...........12
Graham Cracker Caramel Crisps...........69
Nutty Caramel Layer Brownies..............94

CASHEW
Cashew Butter Cookies..........................34

CEREAL
Butter Rum Almond Crunch 9
Cherry Date Skillet Cookies..................10
Chewy Candy Crunch Bars 14
Chocolate-Topped Crunchy Cereal Bars..16
Cookie Jar Cookies 48
No-Bake Rocky Road Chocolate Bars 18

CHEESECAKE
Cheesecake Squares 56

CHERRY
Butter Rum Almond Crunch 9
Cheery Cherry Macaroons.....................27
Cherry Almond Chocolate Bars.............61

Cherry Date Skillet Cookies..................10
Chocolate Drizzled Cherry Bars 104

CHOCOLATE
Chewy Candy Crunch Bars 14
Chocolate Chunk Orange Blonde Brownies...............................85
Crazy-Topped Brownies.........................86
Double Fudge Cream Cheese Brownies................................88
Holiday Chocolate Butter Cookies.......112
Irish Mist Brownies 90
Jumbo Candy & Nut Cookies 44
Mexican Chocolate Wedding Cakes 124
No-Bake Chocolate Cookies 17
Nutty Caramel Layer Brownies..............94
Nutty Chocolate Chunk Cookies...........46
Old-Fashioned Brownies 89
Peppermint N' Chocolate Bars...............22
Rocky Road Fudge Brownies 93
Toffee Candy Bar Brownies 96
Triple Chocolate Fudge Brownies..........92
White & Dark Chocolate Layered Cookies 100

CHOCOLATE CHIP
Caramel N' Chocolate Pecan Bars..........58
Chewy Jumbo Chocolate Chip Cookies......................................31
Chocolate Caramel & Nut Treats...........12
Chocolate Caramel Oatmeal Bars 64
Chocolate Chip Peanut Butter Brownies....................................97
Chocolate Meringue Peanut Bars...........65
Chocolate-Topped Crunchy Cereal Bars..16
Double Fudge Cream Cheese Brownies................................88
English Toffee Bars 76
Grasshopper Butter Cream Bars............66
No-Bake Rocky Road Chocolate Bars 18
Nutty Caramel Layer Brownies..............94
Peanut Brittle Bars..................................74
Peanut Butter Chocolate Bars 78
Peanut Butter Chocolate Chip Bars........80
Peanut Butter Chocolate Granola Bars...19
Peppermint N' Chocolate Bars...............22
Triple Chocolate Fudge Brownies..........92

126

CHOCOLATE WAFER
Orange Butter Cream Squares..................8

CINNAMON
Cinnamon Coffee Cookies...................119
Cinnamon N' Sugar Shortbread 106

COCONUT
Caramel Chew Coconut Bars..................60
Cheery Cherry Macaroons....................27
Cherry Date Skillet Cookies..................10
Cookie Jar Cookies 48
Graham Cracker Caramel Crisps...........69
Lemon Coconut Bars 73
Lemon Doodles......................................42
No-Bake Chocolate Cookies 17
Peanut Butter Chocolate Bars 78
Piña Colada Cookies.............................36

COFFEE
Cinnamon Coffee Cookies...................119
Mocha Almond Bars 77
Triple Chocolate Fudge Brownies 92

COOKIES, see also Bar Cookies;
Brownies; No-Bake Bar Cookies;
No-Bake Cookies

COOKIES, CUT-OUT
Buttery Pistachio Cookies 32
Creamy Lemon Medallions..................110
Czechoslovakian Kolache Cookies 114
Favorite Butter Cookies 116
Teatime Sandwich Cookies..................125

COOKIES, DROP
Buttery Toffee Cookies 30
Cashew Butter Cookies..........................34
Cheery Cherry Macaroons....................27
Chewy Jumbo Chocolate
  Chip Cookies 31
Cookie Jar Cookies 48
Grandma's Cookie Jar
  Oatmeal Cookies 40
Hermits 37
Honey Gems 26
Honey N' Spice Cookies 43
Jumbo Candy & Nut Cookies 44
Lemon Doodles......................................42
Macadamia Nut White Chocolate
  Chunk Cookies 49
Nutty Chocolate Chunk Cookies...........46
Piña Colada Cookies.............................36
Tart N' Tangy Lemonade Frosties..........50

COOKIES, SHAPED
Banana Cream Sandwich Cookies 28
Holiday Thumbprint Cookies 120
Mexican Chocolate Wedding Cakes 124

Snowball Cookies 122
Versatile Butter Cookies 52

COOKIES, REFRIGERATED & MOLDED
Black Walnut Ice Box Cookies............102
Cinnamon Coffee Cookies...................119
Cinnamon N' Sugar Shortbread 106
Citrus Slice N' Bake Cookies.................38
Cranberry Hazelnut Biscotti 108
Holiday Chocolate Butter Cookies.......112
Melt-In-Your-Mouth Spritz 101
White & Dark Chocolate
  Layered Cookies 100

CREAM CHEESE
Double Fudge Cream Cheese
  Brownies...88
Irish Mist Brownies 90

CREME DE MENTHE
Grasshopper Butter Cream Bars.............66

CRANBERRY
Cranberry Hazelnut Biscotti 108

D

DATE
Cherry Date Skillet Cookies..................10
Frosted Orange Date Bars 57

F

FROSTINGS & GLAZES
Applesauce Raisin Bars 103
Caramel Chew Coconut Bars..................60
Cherry Almond Chocolate Bars.............61
Chocolate Drizzled Cherry Bars 104
Cinnamon Coffee Cookies...................119
Crazy-Topped Brownies........................86
Czechoslovakian Kolache Cookies 114
Double Fudge Cream
  Cheese Brownies................................88
Favorite Butter Cookies 116
Frosted Orange Date Bars 57
Frosted Pumpkin Bars 118
Honey Gems 26
Honey N' Spice Cookies 43
Peanut Brittle Bars 74
Peppermint N' Chocolate Bars...............22
Piña Colada Cookies.............................36
Strawberry Marzipan Bars.....................72
Tart N' Tangy Lemonade Frosties..........50
Triple Chocolate Fudge Brownies 92

G

GRAHAM CRACKER
Graham Cracker Caramel Crisps...........69
Microwave Toffee Bars 20

GRANOLA
Peanut Butter Chocolate
  Granola Bars 19

H

HAZELNUT
Cranberry Hazelnut Biscotti 108

HONEY
Cashew Butter Cookies..........................34
Honey Gems 26
Honey N' Spice Cookies 43

L

LEMON
Citrus Slice N' Bake Cookies.................38
Creamy Lemon Medallions..................110
Lemon Coconut Bars 73
Lemon Doodles......................................42
Lemon-Butter Bars 70

LEMONADE
Tart N' Tangy Lemonade Frosties..........50

M

MACADAMIA NUT
Macadamia Nut White Chocolate
  Chunk Cookies 49
Triple Chocolate Fudge Brownies 92

MARSHMALLOW
Butter Rum Almond Crunch 9
Caramel Rocky Road Bars....................62
Graham Cracker Caramel Crisps...........69
No-Bake Rocky Road Chocolate Bars ...18
Peanut Butter No-Bake Cookies 23
Rocky Road Fudge Brownies 93

MERINGUE
Chocolate Meringue Peanut Bars...........65

MOCHA
Mocha Almond Bars 77

MOLASSES
Hermits 37

127

N

NO-BAKE BAR COOKIES
Butter Rum Almond Crunch 9
Chewy Candy Crunch Bars 14
Chocolate Caramel & Nut Treats..........12
Chocolate-Topped Crunchy
　Cereal Bars..................................16
Microwave Toffee Bars 20
No-Bake Rocky Road Chocolate Bars....18
Orange Butter Cream Squares.................8
Peanut Butter Chocolate
　Granola Bars 19
Peppermint N' Chocolate Bars..............22

NO-BAKE COOKIES
Cherry Date Skillet Cookies...................10
No-Bake Chocolate Cookies 17
Peanut Butter No-Bake Cookies 23

O

OAT
Caramel Rocky Road Bars......................62
Chocolate Caramel Oatmeal Bars 64
Chocolate Drizzled Cherry Bars 104
Cookie Jar Cookies 48
Grandma's Cookie Jar
　Oatmeal Cookies 40
Honey Gems 26
Jumbo Candy & Nut Cookies 44
No-Bake Chocolate Cookies 17
Peanut Butter No-Bake Cookies 23

ORANGE
Chocolate Chunk Orange
　Blonde Brownies...........................85
Cinnamon Coffee Cookies...................119
Citrus Slice N' Bake Cookies.................38
Favorite Butter Cookies 116
Frosted Orange Date Bars 57
Honey Gems 26
Honey N' Spice Cookies 43
Orange Butter Cream Squares.................8

P

PEANUT
Chewy Candy Crunch Bars 14
Chocolate Caramel & Nut Treats...........12
Chocolate Meringue Peanut Bars 65
Chocolate-Topped Crunchy
　Cereal Bars..................................16
Jumbo Candy & Nut Cookies 44
Peanut Brittle Bars................................74

Peanut Butter Chocolate Chip Bars........80
Peanut Butter Squares...........................81
Rocky Road Fudge Brownies 93

PEANUT BUTTER
Chocolate Chip Peanut Butter
　Brownies.......................................97
Peanut Butter Chocolate Bars 78
Peanut Butter Chocolate Chip Bars........80
Peanut Butter Chocolate
　Granola Bars 19
Peanut Butter No-Bake Cookies 23
Peanut Butter Squares...........................81

PECANS
Caramel Chew Coconut Bars................60
Caramel N' Chocolate Pecan Bars.........58
Cheery Cherry Macaroons 27
Chocolate Caramel Oatmeal Bars 64
English Toffee Bars...............................76
Nutty Caramel Layer Brownies..............94
Old-World Raspberry Bars....................68
Snowball Cookies 122

PEPPERMINT
Peppermint N' Chocolate Bars..............22
Snow-Topped Peppermint Bars...........113

PINEAPPLE
Piña Colada Cookies............................36

PISTACHIO
Buttery Pistachio Cookies 32

PRESERVES
Czechoslovakian Kolache Cookies 114
Old-World Raspberry Bars....................68
Piña Colada Cookies............................36
Strawberry Marzipan Bars.....................72

PUMPKIN
Frosted Pumpkin Bars 118

R

RAISIN
Applesauce Raisin Bars 103
Frosted Pumpkin Bars 118
Hermits...37

RASPBERRY
Old-World Raspberry Bars....................68

RUM
Butter Rum Almond Crunch 9
Piña Colada Cookies............................36

S

SESAME SEED
Honey Gems 26

SHORTBREAD
Cinnamon N' Sugar Shortbread 106

SPRITZ
Melt-In-Your-Mouth Spritz 101

STRAWBERRY
Strawberry Marzipan Bars.....................72

T

TOFFEE
Buttery Toffee Cookies 30
English Toffee Bars...............................76
Microwave Toffee Bars 20
Toffee Candy Bar Brownies 96

W

WALNUT
Black Walnut Ice Box Cookies............102
Cookie Jar Cookies 48
Hermits...37
Nutty Chocolate Chunk Cookies..........46
Old-Fashioned Brownies 89

WHITE CHOCOLATE
Fruit-Filled White
　Chocolate Brownies.......................84
Macadamia Nut White Chocolate
　Chunk Cookies 49
White & Dark Chocolate
　Layered Cookies 100

Y

YEAST
Czechoslovakian Kolache Cookies 114